MEN'S RIGHTS
A HANDBOOK FOR THE 80'S

Also by William R. Wishard and Laurie Wishard
ADOPTION: The Grafted Tree

Also by William R. Wishard
Rights of the Elderly & Retired

MEN'S RIGHTS
A HANDBOOK FOR THE 80'S

WILLIAM R. WISHARD, LL.B.
AND
LAURIE WISHARD, M.S.W.

cragmont publications

MEN'S RIGHTS

Published by
Cragmont Publications
161 Berry Street, Suite 6410
San Francisco, California 94107

Manufactured in the United States of America
First printing August 1980

Editor: Diane Sipes
Editorial advisor: Pauline McGuire
Project coordinator: Fred E. Felder
Design: Carolyn Bean Associates, Incorporated
Proofreader: Kathleen Hartley
Typesetting: Medallion Graphics
Printing & binding: George Banta Company, Inc.

Library of Congress Cataloging in Publication Data

Wishard, William R   1930–
    Men's rights.

    Bibliography: p.
    Includes index.
    1. Men — Legal status, laws, etc. — United States.
2. Divorce — United States.   I. Wishard, Laurie,
1948–   joint author.   II. Title.
KF475.W57   346.7301'3   80-20194
ISBN 0-89666-012-5 (pbk.)
ISBN 0-89666-011-7

A Note to the Reader

Contents

PART II
DIVORCE AND SEPARATION:
THE PARTNERS

PART III
DIVORCE AND SEPARATION: THE CHILD

PART I

YESTERDAY AND TODAY: CHALLENGES AND CHOICES

1
Equality: Balancing the Scales

*In January 1970, Joe left home for his job as a salesman, as he had
done every morning for the past ten years. He had a wife, two kids,
a mortgage, a car, and a cat to support.*

*Two years later his house was a mess, his children screaming, and
his wife bored and unfulfilled. She went back to school to find herself,
and Joe still went to work. Later his wife found herself, a career,
and a more understanding lover. And Joe found an apartment.
Now Joe pays half his salary to support the children he sees only twice
a month. He still goes to work every day, but now he is called
a salesperson.*

Joe and some of the guys from the office meet at a bar
almost every night now after work. Over a few beers, they
reminisce about the good old days when men were men and
women were women. They exchange wisecracks about
women's lib, and everybody has a good laugh. Some of the
men — the ones who still have a wife and family — watch
the clock casually. When they leave, Joe feels sad and angry.
He also feels lonely. But what the hell — the crazy way things
are going these days, what's a guy to do?

Besides Joe, there are executives sitting alone in their
offices, bitter and worried because they can't make sense out
of life anymore. And carpenters, swearing as they drive in
nails, trying to forget that their wives and girlfriends have
left them. And lawyers who blame their failing marriages on
wives who "don't know when they've got it made." And
truckdrivers who plan to go to Mexico where women still
understand men. And so on.

What has brought about this winter of men's discontent? Much of the answer lies in what has happened to women during the last ten years.

The Seventies: Changing of the Guard

The women's movement arrived in 1970, and by the end of the decade things were never to be the same again. Vietnam was more dramatic; Watergate attracted more attention. But the women's movement became a permanent part of our national consciousness.

After centuries of playing supporting parts, women joined ranks and decided to increase their repertoire of roles. They entered the company of the actors, the breadwinners, and the decision-makers — parts that had hitherto been reserved for men.

Women organized, worked, and fought, and the results were startling. Discrimination on the basis of sex in employment, education, credit, and other civil matters was outlawed. Affirmative Action programs and training opportunities were enacted and implemented to ensure women's access to the business world. Small business loans and other state and federal monies were made available to interested women. And, of course, employers were educated as to their responsibility for women's entry into the job market.

Women, out to make a place for themselves in the world, also had to liberate themselves from many home duties. Now contraception and abortion-on-demand have freed them from unwanted children, and husbands and partners are being educated as to their equal responsibility for child-care and housework.

Women have also been liberated from the social expectation that they must be good wives and mothers. Women can and do choose to leave marriage and motherhood — or never enter into either. Children can be responsibly delegated to day-care centers, their fathers, or even to governmental agencies.

In short, women now have options and the power to exercise those options. The women's movement will certainly continue to grow, and there are battles yet to be won. Still, it seems fair to say that *equality* for women is a reality as we enter the eighties — an incomplete reality, many would argue, but nevertheless a tangible one.

Meanwhile, Back at the Ranch . . .

For many men, the women's movement has left in its wake confusion, bitterness, and hostility. Many relationships were fractured, many families disintegrated, and many people are now haunted by a pervasive sense of loss — women as well as men. The movement also left behind a confused legal system that is still struggling to pick up the pieces.

The effects of women's liberation have been felt by every man in one way or another. For every Alice who didn't live there anymore, a man riding the 5:15 as he had done for years, his paycheck already spoken for, wondered where *he* lived. "Women aren't all cute little Blondies," proclaimed the new woman. "Well," thought men, "*we* aren't all bumbling Dagwoods, either."

A few men saw that the women's movement might spin off benefits for men. If women could have freedom of choice, so could men. If female stereotypes were to be discarded, perhaps male stereotypes could also be shattered. And this has proved to be true — for some.

But how did men respond to the challenge posed by the women's movement? With a deafening silence. Only very recently has the male voice been heard in the land on its own behalf — and then not very loudly.

Why have men been unwilling or unable to respond effectively to the new woman? One reason is certainly guilt. Men must concede that women were indeed victimized by various forms of discrimination and to some extent still are. Fine and good, says the woman of the eighties, but with guilty friends, who needs enemies?

Another important reason for men's passivity to these sweeping changes is that men tend to be loners in their personal lives. Seldom will men willingly share their doubts, their dreams, or their confusion and anger, except perhaps with their family. As a result, a man's personal identification is generally based on his accomplishments ("I'm an engineer — a physician — a teamster") or his interests as a member of a group ("I'm a Mason — a golfer — a Democrat — a baseball fan"). In general, a *man's* identification with *men* hinges on such connections, rather than on his male individuality.

It follows that men generally have been oblivious to or disinterested in *men's causes* (with the possible exception of war). Perhaps this was understandable — even logical — before the women's movement changed their lives. It is less understandable as we enter the eighties, and certainly less logical. Women are legitimately exerting tremendous pressures on lawmakers and the courts to establish and protect their interests as they see them. But what men's organization do *you* know of that has the clout of NOW (National Organization of Women)? For that matter, what men's organizations (other than special interest groups) do you *know* of? Here and there a few such groups are emerging, but by and large they are voices in the wilderness.

Contrast such apathy with the vigor and power of the women's movement. In varying degrees, it has raised the consciousness of most women to pride in their sex and awareness of the problems and goals connected with it. Even though the movement has failed to persuade *all* women to accept each of the movement's contentions, still it is the rare adult female who has not heard its call. Names like Betty Friedan, Germaine Greer, Shirley Chisholm, Barbara Jordan, Bella Abzug, Jane Fonda — "Hall of Famers" whose names ring bells everywhere. Can you think of any male equivalents?

Equality — Balancing the Scales

Personal feelings or paralysis notwithstanding, most of us who are interested in survival eventually *do* shake off our lethargy, have a look around, and see what's coming down. Then we decide what we can do about it. And that translates into what our rights are. By and large, women's rights have now been defined by our laws and implemented by them. How do men, in the eighties, re-define their rights? Have men's rights been bypassed or brushed aside by the courts and the legislatures in their preoccupation with women's liberation?

Family Matters In family matters men remain the victims of tradition. In days gone by men had a reasonable duty to their families; women needed protection and economic security; their lives, their interests, and their place was at home; and the law mirrored this. When a relationship went sour, women still needed protection, and men still had to provide it. Since the role of women has changed so drastically, the continued enforcement of these traditional male roles means nothing less than discrimination against men.

The recent award-winning film, *Kramer vs. Kramer,* points out the legal inequality that sadly remains in family matters. While some states treat men equally in theory, in practice women still retain an iron grip on child custody and the plums of child support, alimony, and generous property settlements.

Women, regardless of their situations, are generally presumed to be economically disadvantaged when compared to men. The courts routinely require men to shoulder support payments and to concede a lion's share of the family property when marriages end. The obligation of women to support themselves and their families, when occasionally recognized, is seldom enforced on an equal basis.

A man forever suffers the disadvantage of never experiencing pregnancy. Since he never can become pregnant, he is barred from deciding whether or not to abort his child. He can never establish that "sacred maternal bond beginning in the womb" that often gives women preference in custody decisions. In states that do provide men some equality in custody matters, men frequently must be twice as competent as women in order to be considered equal. For every Dr. Salk who wins custody of his children, there are tens of fathers who lose, and hundreds of fathers who are too discouraged to fight.

7

This leaves men still out in the cold and looking in at the hearth. A man's place in the family circle is dependent on the women in his life.

The law has not kept pace with the realities of the eighties. Most states still retain 1920 vintage family law that presumes men to be breadwinners and women to be babymakers. And most courts still tend to view men as support evaders rather than as individuals and serious parents. But there is now a trend toward abolishing these stereotypes, "de-sexing" family law, and equalizing the rights and responsibilities of men and women.

This, though, is only a trend, and one that seems very shallow to a father fighting for the custody of his child. To make this trend become a norm, lawmakers must be prodded to legislate equality, and courts must be presented with cases by men attempting to affirm their rights to equality.

In Economics The major thrust of the women's movement has been and still is to achieve financial equality. By 1972 the battle for legal equality in employment, education, and citizenship had already been won; women had the same legal rights and opportunities as men.

But this brand of equality did not address women's most important concern — getting their "rightful" share of power and economic benefits. The women's movement tied its fortunes to those of the ethnic minorities, and as a result 100 million American women became the beneficiaries of preferential treatment in employment and education.

The theory behind this preferential treatment is that women and minorities have been discriminated against in the past. So the lawmakers changed the rules of the game to discriminate against the discriminators, which led to the state of confusion we are experiencing today.

The courts are bound by the principle of equality before the law. Once women had secured protection from sexual discrimination, men were entitled to the same protection.

The courts were uncomfortable with this challenge. Should they defend the honor of legal equality or give women, minorities, and the disadvantaged a needed break?

With the steadfastness of marshmallow knights, they deliberated, equivocated, and remained confused. The result is a legal muddle that is equally unsatisfactory to all.

So where does this leave men? Today the ugly reality of limited job opportunities and promotions makes preferential treatment for any single group a bread-and-butter issue. In order for a woman to obtain her "rightful" share of the pie, someone else may have to settle for less. And the discouraged male job seeker reading work applications that encourage women and minorities to apply may well feel that he is that someone. A new kind of inequality has entered the picture.

How Can This Book Help?

This book is pro-men; it is not anti-women or anti-family. The authors are father and daughter, one born in the good old days, the other in the brave new world. We believe in true equality but hope we never lose the ability to laugh at ourselves in the process.

We are also convinced that men's rights, their needs and interests, have been unpopular and unmentionable subjects in recent years. Men have been their own worst advocates, sitting by passively watching their lives erode.

Men and women need each other, need to live together, work together, and share their lives and their children. Both are entitled to their rights. And neither should be exempt from their responsibilities. Women's rights cannot mean that women are the only beneficiaries of equality.

This book examines the problems men experience as individuals and in their relationships with women and children. Some legal guidelines for defining and solving these problems are suggested and explained in non-legalese. Other sources and materials dealing with these problems are included in the appendix and bibliography at the end of the book.

2
Marriage: The Blank Contract

We take each other to love and to cherish, in sickness and in health, for better or for worse, until death do us part.

These beautiful sentiments are called marriage vows. Presumably, the persons making them intend their union to be permanent for life. During the seventies, however, over half of all legal marriages failed.

This chapter examines some of the reasons why the traditional marriage agreement doesn't work for many men and makes some suggestions for change. The advantages and disadvantages of marriage as opposed to alternative relationships are outlined, as well as some practical proposals on premarital agreements and property inventories.

Marriage — A Contract?

Don and Becky have lived together for a while and are thinking of making it legal. If they do, they plan on tearing up a written agreement they made that spells out the terms and conditions of their relationship. Don wonders whether their relationship will be the same after they marry.

Judges and lawyers have argued for years over the question of whether marriage is a contract in the legal sense. The consensus seems to be that marriage is a *status* or an *institution*, but not a contract.

Still, marriage has much in common with a contract: both persons must consent to be married and must be legally capable of giving consent (they must be of age, and so on); if a marriage agreement is based on fraud (if one of the persons was already married, for example), the marriage may be rescinded (annulled), as in other contracts; and items of tangible value (rings) are usually exchanged, as in other contracts.

But, unlike other agreements we enter into — such as business partnership agreements — the *rights and duties* of the marriage agreement are not specified. The promises made by the parties are unwritten and often not even spoken. In fact, it is questionable whether many persons entering into marriage even know what rights and duties are involved.

If marriage isn't a contract, then, how do the persons involved know what to expect from their partners? How are the respective rights and duties of married persons defined? The answer is — by the law of domestic relations (often called family law). This law is the means by which each state regulates and controls the institution of marriage.

To better understand what a legal marriage is and is not, a brief look at the history of marriage as an institution may be helpful.

Background

Traditional marriage was a civil, religious, and economic institution of common law (English law). Upon marriage, the husband and wife were merged into the legal identity of the husband. He was the family's head — its agent — as well as the economic, legal, and personal decision maker of the household.

A woman, when she married, lost control of her property and the right to make a contract in her own name, and, if she worked, her husband was entitled to the management and control of her earnings. If a woman was divorced under common law, she had a right to have her property returned to her.

Under common law, the husband was completely responsible for the support of his wife and children. In return, the wife rendered services in the home, maintained it with the resources furnished by the husband, and cared for the children. The duties of husband and wife complemented each other. This was a simple, permanent, workable way of living — in those days.

But by the mid nineteenth century, common law no longer reflected social and economic realities. Each state was beginning to enact its own family law, and those laws are still changing today.

Recent Changes in the Law

The institution of marriage has eroded rapidly over the last ten or twenty years. For many people, marriage is no longer a necessity or even a desirable choice. Women are no longer as economically dependent on men as they once were, and contraception and abortion make childbearing an option rather than an inevitability.

Sex and parenthood outside of marriage are becoming more and more widely accepted. Men and women are increasingly opting to live together unmarried rather than, or before becoming, married.

The lawmakers have responded to these social changes by changing domestic law. These changes, of course, have been uneven throughout the states and are still in progress. But generally speaking, it has become much easier and less financially disastrous to end a marriage. The distinctions between men and women in domestic law are diminishing, so that men now have a better chance of getting custody of their children and not paying alimony. Lawmakers have recognized that great numbers of unmarried men and women are living together and having children together. The courts of many states will recognize the agreements made by couples living together and, at times, treat these couples as if they were married. Increasingly, states provide that illegitimate children (and their fathers) have the same rights as legitimate children.

But these new laws, for the most part, have modernized only what happens when a marriage fails; they have not given us a new legal formula for how a marriage should work.

Brides and grooms still "gather in the sight of God," or at least of their friends, and make promises very similar to those made by their forebearers.

Marriage as a Choice

Marriage is now only one of the choices that men have. It is equally normal, acceptable, and practical for many men never to marry, to end a marriage, to be unmarried and have sexual relationships, to live with a woman, to live with a man, to be childless, and to be unmarried and have a child.

For a variety of reasons, marriage has become less necessary from a practical point of view. Often it is advantageous in terms of dollars and cents *not* to marry. Marriage can result in the loss of pensions and retirement, in paying more taxes, and in immense monetary obligations to an ex-spouse. Furthermore, many states allow couples who live together to draw up agreements that are more (or less) binding than marriage. Most important, these agreements can be tailored to an individual couple's specific situation.

However, neither these practical reasons, nor the legal erosion of the institution of marriage, nor the widespread acceptance of living together have stopped men from making the trip to the altar. Yet men are freer from the pressure to do so. Fewer men are asked to make women "honest," or asked to "give their child a father," or promised sex in return for marriage.

Marriage, for all its faults and failings, still has a very powerful religious and symbolic value; it is a public commitment a man and woman make to live their lives together. That marriage does have an "out-clause," that it doesn't clearly specify what's expected, and that it means different things to different people are, perhaps, not that important. It does provide the *hope* of security and commitment, and that often seems to be enough.

And perhaps men need this commitment now as much as, if not more than, women. All of us are complicated, vulnerable creatures, who probably find real intimacy with another person the most difficult proposition of our lives.

Men can no longer assume that their financially dependent wives will "tough it out" with them. At the same time, men are being asked to risk more — to be vulnerable and tender with their wives and to be equal, nurturing parents. Their female partners are liable to be their equals in work, competence, education, sex, and intelligence. Since men must now risk more, with more formidable partners perhaps, they too need the protection of a secure commitment.

The Rights and Responsibilities of Married People

The marriage ceremony and vows still reflect traditional common law and still form the basis for the modern institution of marriage. But do these vows have a legal meaning any longer? Can they be relied upon? And, do they even vaguely reflect what you might want from marriage?

". . . joined together . . ." You may have promised to bind yourself into a "mystical union." But the law first recognizes you and your wife as *independent individuals,* and only second as a husband and wife obligated to each other. As the U.S. Supreme Court put it when legalizing abortion, "traditional state control of the marital status has had to give way to current notions of individual liberty and the right to privacy." [*Roe vs. Wade 410 US 113*].

Husband and wife are now seen more as two separate individuals, who during their marriage voluntarily share parts of their lives rather than as a permanent economic, social, and legal unit. Most of the changes in marital rights and obligations have followed from this change in thinking.

You own your own body and have your own personal rights and freedoms — and so does your wife. For the most part, whatever either of you do for the other is done voluntarily, not because of any legally enforceable duty to each other.

There is, naturally, an exception to this general trend: when money is the issue, you can expect the bonds of matrimony to be quite tight. Marital obligations are enforced in order to prevent a spouse from becoming a burden to the taxpayer.

"... man and wife ..." These days, couples are seldom pronounced "man and wife." "Husband and wife" is the modern idiom. And this change in ceremony parallels a change in the law.

In the past, a man was the head of the household to the extent that he nearly owned his wife. His authority over his wife was similar to the authority parents now have over their children. However, in more recent times a man's role became simply that of legal decision maker in such matters as investing the family money and determining the family residence.

Times have changed. You are no longer head of your household. You and your wife share authority to make decisions and have no authority over each other's actions. When your two heads don't agree, you can compromise, live with it, or divorce. And that's it.

"... with all my worldly goods, I thee endow ..." These are the traditional words of the husband as he places the ring on his wife's finger and assumes the traditional obligation to support her. This is an obligation that has survived the test of time.

Every state still requires a husband to support his wife during their marriage and sometimes, depending on circumstances, after a marriage. The laws of a few states still require the husband to assume the primary duty to support his family. However, all states provide that in some instances a wife must support her husband and most states give spouses equal responsibility to support each other. Unfortunately, a wife's equal obligation to support her husband is rarely enforced.

Our advice to you: Insist on a double ring ceremony.

"... obey him and serve him ..." This was the first offensive item to be red-pencilled out of the marriage vows. Originally, this vow affirmed a woman's acceptance of her

husband's authority and her willingness to contribute to the marriage by maintaining her husband's household. It complemented her husband's promise to support her and their family.

Legally, your wife is not required to accept your authority. Nor does your opinion carry any more weight than hers. Furthermore, you and your wife are both just as obligated to care for your children, clean the bathroom, and walk the dog.

"*. . . to have and to hold . . .*" Having and holding your wife may be your hope, but it is not your right. Sex is no longer a married man's right; even in marriage, sex remains a voluntary act. In fact, a growing number of states now classify a husband's forcing his wife to have sex with him as rape.

Nor can you demand that your wife make you a father. Formerly, courts considered that "one of the leading and most important objects of the institution of marriage under our law is the procreation of children . . ." [*Reynolds vs. Reynolds 85 Mass 610*]. Your wife, however, can refuse to have children, make use of contraception and abortion, and be sterilized without your consent or even notification. But, for whatever it's worth, you have the same rights.

The law still recognizes that having a sexual relationship and having children is part of marriage. While you can never force your wife to have either with you, you can divorce her for not doing so. And, should your wife feel that you are denying her children or the pleasures of your body, she of course has the same option.

"*. . . forsaking all others . . .*" This is many couples' intention, but again it is not legally enforceable. If your wife forgets to forsake the others, you can divorce her. In most states, the adultery of your wife will not affect a property settlement, spousal support, child support, or even child custody.

The result may be somewhat different if you are the "sinning" spouse. Some states can still require men to pay in alimony for their "sins." Moral: What's sauce for the goose is not always sauce for the gander.

". . . til death us do part . . ." It is certainly true that death is no longer the only salvation from a miserable marriage. The majority of states allow either a husband or a wife to divorce for any reason and without the spouse's consent. Some states still require grounds for divorce, but even in these states ingenious (and well-off) spouses can easily find ways to divorce.

And increasingly there is no legal penalty for divorce. The courts simply try to divide up the family property and allocate support as best they can. Wives and husbands are less and less being financially punished for not keeping their promises.

". . . to love and to cherish . . ." Again, beautiful sentiments. But this is not, and never was, a legally enforceable promise.

When a Marriage Works — The Legal Problems

Everyone has problems when a marriage fails. In fact, we devote two-thirds of this book (Parts II and III) to these problems. However, even marriages that succeed in a personal sense don't necessarily escape the failings of the modern institution of marriage. Many couples happily live their married lives together, but after the death of one of the partners, the other is faced with many of the same problems as in marriages that end in divorce.

And, naturally, these problems concern money and property. The law cannot and will not involve itself in the personal relationship between a husband and wife. But upon death or divorce, the law decides what is his, hers, theirs, and the government's.

A traditional marriage, supported by the family law in your state, may work well for you, or it may not suit your particular needs at all. For example, if you are twenty-three years old and plan to marry a woman of about the same age, rear a family, work and save for a house, and grow old with your wife, general family law will probably work very well.

But consider the following examples:

Ralph is 46, has a business, three children by a former marriage, a house, and pays spousal support. He wants to marry Susan, aged 53, who has two grown children, a job, a house, and pension rights from her former husband.

Alex, 69, is a well-off widower, father of seven and grandfather of twenty. His bride-to-be is 62, has some severe medical problems, and lives on social security and SSI income.

Obviously the flexibility of marriage is called into question, as well as the ability of people to tailor it to suit their own particular needs and circumstances. In these two examples, Ralph and Alex are older, have been married before and have prior obligations as well as considerable property. The typical marriage agreement (as well as family law in general) does *not* reflect the realities of their situations or even their intentions.

If you are a man who wants to marry but, because of your particular situation, doubt that the traditional marriage agreement will work for you, what can or should you do? The remainder of this chapter discusses some ways you can help yourself and still be fair to your wife.

Before You Marry — Premarital Agreements

A premarital agreement (often called an antenuptial agreement or a marriage settlement agreement) is a written contract entered into by a prospective husband and a prospective wife. The agreement is made *before* marriage, but it may be effective either before or after the persons are married, depending on what they want.

Do *not* confuse premarital agreements either with living-together agreements (agreements *in lieu of marriage*) or with marital separation agreements by married persons after they have separated or divorced.

Purpose A premarital agreement enables each prospective married partner to specify what property he or she owns before marriage, what property he or she might own after marriage, and what he or she intends to do with the property.

The immense advantage of making such an agreement before you marry is that it provides a fair and equitable basis for the division and distribution of the property of each person should the marriage fail or one person die. The costly and often bitter property battles that sometimes follow divorce are largely avoided by such agreements.

Drafting a premarital agreement is not a very romantic task. It forces both of you to face up to the disagreeable fact that your marriage eventually will end, and that both of you are concerned with your individual interests. Avoiding these facts will not make them disappear. Either the domestic relations court or the probate court will eventually sort out your property. Premarital agreements will help make that settlement fair and one that you and your future wife want. On the bright side, this agreement may allow you and your bride to begin your marriage without the threat of money and property disputes.

What Premarital Agreements Cannot Do A premarital agreement will *not* allow you to write your own marriage contract. You'd better decide before you marry how the housekeeping will be divided, the income spent, whether you want children, and so on.

A premarital agreement *may not change the personal marital rights* that the law gives to married persons or their children. For example:

Ralph and Susan plan on marriage. The state where they are to be married has a law imposing on a husband the duty to support his wife. Ralph and Susan sign an agreement in which Susan waives her right to support when they are married. That part of the agreement is not valid.

Similarly:

Dan and Maria make a premarital agreement in which Maria agrees that if the marriage fails Dan will have no duty to support any children of the marriage. The agreement is no good — every state imposes such a duty on a father if the child requires support.

Agreements such as this one are considered by the courts to be made "in contemplation of divorce" and are not valid. The reasoning is that such an agreement encourages or facilitates divorce, which is against public policy.

There are some exceptions to the above rule. For example, a Florida court upheld an agreement that provided $600 a month alimony to the wife in the event of divorce. Similar examples are found in Nevada, Oregon, and California. Still, by and large you would be well advised to avoid such agreements; in most cases your wife can break them.

However, consider the following example:

Milt and Carolyn make a premarital agreement in which Carolyn agrees to waive her community property rights in exchange for Milt's promise to give her $10,000. This agreement is valid since no personal rights are involved — only property rights.

When Is a Premarital Agreement Recommended or Necessary? We recommend premarital agreements for all couples planning marriage, but for some couples they are absolutely necessary. If any of the following is true for either yourself or your future wife, you will need an agreement.

- You have a substantial amount of property or money, or expect to receive either of these soon.
- One of you earns or has much more money or property than the other.
- You have children.
- You have debts or monetary obligations.
- You own a business.
- You had a longstanding previous marriage.
- You have pension rights.
- You own something or are in a partnership with another person.
- You are living together.
- You are in a complicated tax situation.
- You will give up something of value, such as a job, for the marriage.

How to Make a Premarital Agreement The *technicalities* of a valid premarital agreement in most states are as follows:

(1) the agreement must be in writing; (2) it must be signed by both persons; (3) it must be acknowledged (before witnesses); and (4) it must usually be notarized and recorded in the county where it was made.

A form for a premarital agreement is not included in this book. It is doubtful whether any form would be legally suitable for all states. We suggest that if you need a premarital agreement, it is worth the expense to have an attorney draw one up for you.

For your assistance, however, here is a tentative checklist of items that should be included in most premarital agreements:

- the names and addresses of each prospective spouse (including all the names under which either person has gone in the past, such as former married or maiden name)
- a description of the property owned by each person
- the approximate value of the property owned by each person
- if one person is transferring property to the other or to the marriage community, an itemization of the property and its value
- a statement concerning the ownership of property that either person may acquire after marriage (by gift, will, and so on)
- provisions covering the transfer of property and termination of the agreement if either party dies
- release of marital property rights
- provisions for benefits to or the support of children of a former marriage or a former spouse or relatives
- a statement as to the effect of termination of the marriage (other than by death)
- a statement that each person has fully and honestly disclosed all of his or her property
- a statement that each person has given up something of value in reliance on the other person's promise (called "consideration")
- provisions for changing, revoking, or terminating the agreement (such as the return of property if the parties fail to marry)

• the date the agreement was signed and the date it is effective
• a statement that the agreement is not made in contemplation of divorce or separation

Warning: Be sure to check the requirements of your own state as to filing, recording, and so on. The clerk of the family law court should be able to assist you with this.

After Marriage — Property Inventory

A property inventory is simply a list describing what property you and your wife own separately and what property you own jointly. (Different states use different terms for separate and joint property, but they amount to the same thing.) This list is *signed by each of you,* and each of you keeps a copy. You may have already prepared a similar inventory for your insurance agent.

Basically, your separate property is whatever you owned before your marriage and whatever you receive during your marriage by gift, will, or without your expending *any* effort. This property you own totally, and your spouse has no right to it and no control over what you do with it.

Joint property is property that is acquired during your marriage as the result of the efforts of either yourself or your wife. Both of you have a share of this property and some right to control it. The size of each share and the degree of control varies depending on the state you live in.

It seems simple. However, suppose your wife inherits $10,000, and this money is put into a business that you alone run. Is this money a gift to you? A gift to your marriage? Is your wife making a loan to you, personally? A loan to your marriage? Or is she buying a share of your business?

And who owns the business, anyway? You? Your wife? Both of you? These questions are simple enough to make your lawyer rich. The solution: You and your wife can agree when you make the property inventory who owns the business and how you will consider her $10,000 inheritance.

You should make a property inventory at the beginning of your marriage, periodically (at least every five years), and whenever your joint or individual financial circumstances change.

Note that debts are considered to be property and should be included in the inventory. If they are, a creditor may be unable to touch the separate property of the spouse who is not a debtor or even that part of the joint property that is his or hers.

Making a property inventory is a relatively easy proposition, particularly if you have made a premarital agreement or a previous inventory. Simply update the items on the previous list or agreement and add any new items.

If the inventory is your first and you have no premarital agreement, use the following procedure:

• List each item of property owned by each person.
• Indicate where the property came from.
• State where the property is now.
• Assign an agreed-on value to the property.
• Sign and date the agreement and have it notarized.
• Give a copy to your spouse.

If you're in doubt as to the format, ask your insurance agent for an insurance inventory form and use it as a guide.

Remember, your property inventory states what you own, and it may be used in court to protect your interests. You must be sure that it is correct, and that it is fair to both you and your wife. In order to do this, both of you must be aware of the property and inheritance law, as well as the domestic relations law of your state. When a transaction is complicated or involves a good deal of money, we advise you to have an attorney check out your inventory.

One of the difficult and often unavoidable problems in a marriage is that one spouse may sacrifice his or her own career or personal goals for the good of the marriage. Mary leaves her job and for ten years cares for the family while her husband pursues his career. Sam works as a stock clerk in order to put his wife through medical school. If Sam and Mary both stay married to their separate spouses, there will be no problems. Both will share in the benefits of their partner's career and education. But they will both be in financial trouble if their marriage breaks up.

You may be able to agree with your wife as to how much such contributions are worth and include them in the inventory, but remember: you *cannot* use such a provision as a substitute for possible spousal support should your marriage fail.

Buying and Registering Automobiles

You and your wife may register a car in any way you wish, even though both of you may be required to sign the financing papers to buy it. If you intend that the car should be yours only, register it that way (or vice-versa for your wife). But if you intend that the car should be owned jointly by you and your wife, it should be registered jointly under one of the methods outlined below.

• John Black *or* Jane Black
  Joint tenancy means that if one person dies the other gets the car without any legal proceedings. Either person can sell the car without the other's knowledge or consent.
• John Black *and* Jane Black
  Tenancy in common means that both persons have to sign to have the car sold or transferred. If one person dies, the other obtains the car by legal process (usually probate proceedings).
• John Black *and* Jane Black, JTRS
  Joint Tenancy with Right of Survivorship means the same thing as no. 2 above, except that if one person dies the survivor may obtain title to the car from the Department of Motor Vehicles with no further legal complications.

Joint Bank Accounts

A man may open a joint bank account with his wife or, for that matter, with his unmarried partner. If both persons sign the necessary signature cards, they are equally liable for any checks written on the account, even if one of them disappears with all of the money.

Credit and Credit Purchases by Married People

The rules of the credit game have changed considerably in the last few years. Now a woman as well as a man can open any credit account in her own name (including her maiden name if she wishes) and incur liabilities separate from her husband and his consent — or even from his knowledge in many instances.

In some respects, the new laws governing credit benefit men as well as women. A man may apply for credit or a loan under his own name without the consent or signature of his wife (unless she is required to co-sign as a matter of security for the loan).

Except for the fact that neither husband nor wife can diminish the other's separate property by their individual actions, both sexes are now equally free to make the same mistakes and burden their own individual paychecks.

Obtaining Credit; Credit Ratings Under federal law, a creditor cannot discriminate against you on the basis of your marital status. A creditor may *ask* whether you are married or single in order to find out what his or her rights are and how the claim may be enforced. But the information may not be used in any other way.

A creditor may require you to furnish information on any alimony or child support payments you make. These obligations bear directly on your credit-worthiness. But a creditor may not discriminate against you just because you have changed your marital status. This rule is intended to help women, primarily, but it also is and will be of help to men.

Charge Accounts and Cards If you and your wife have signed credit card applications, both of you are equally responsible for all charges by either of you. Furthermore, both of you are equally liable for charges that are made with the consent of either of you.

Harold and Kathy each have a Visa card, for which they each signed. Kathy lets her brother use hers, and he runs up charges to the limit and goes to Texas. Both Harold and Kathy are liable for his charges.

If you want to avoid this type of situation, arrange it so that both of your signatures are required for charges.

Co-signing   Your wife or girlfriend opens a charge account in her name only. But the merchant asks you to co-sign the account, to secure the credit. Are you liable if she doesn't pay? Yes.

Notifying Creditors of Closing of Account   You've probably seen small ads in newspapers and magazines stating that a husband is no longer liable for his wife's bills after a given date. Forget it; such notices may have their purposes, but they won't get you off the hook if that is your intention.

If your marriage is about to break up and you want to stop all credit accounts, you must notify every creditor with whom you have signed an application *to close that account*. Otherwise you are still liable for all charges made against the account even if your marriage has ended.

3
Living Together: Marvin vs. Marvin

Time magazine reported in 1979 (July 9, p. 55) that, according to Census Bureau figures, the number of couples living together unmarried more than doubled in the seventies. There are more than 1,100,000 unmarried couples today in the United States. Living together is no longer just an alternative lifestyle, a counter-culture phenomenon, or something that other people do. It is a widely accepted way for men and women to live and have a relationship.

As is generally true of married persons, the rights and duties of people who live together are defined only when the relationship ends. And the daily newspapers and court dockets reflect the rapidly increasing number of unmarried couples who have disagreements that result in lawsuits.

Some of these couples have claimed that an agreement was made between them, as in the famous *Marvin vs. Marvin* case, which is discussed later in this chapter. Other couples have claimed no such agreement but nevertheless demanded that the courts straighten out their personal and property rights after separation.

When fairness demands, the courts, using various legal fictions, have been willing to determine the property interests of unmarried couples who have made no agreement to live together. But they have shunned living-together agreements, viewing them as illegal, immoral, and in derogation of marriage. The majority of states still hold this view.

But as institutions and attitudes change, so does the law —

29

slowly. Living-together agreements are becoming accepted in more and more states and, when properly tailored to the circumstances, may prove to be a useful means of defining responsibilities in a non-marital relationship.

First, here are some distinctions to keep in mind. Two people who are now described as "living together" have traditionally been called a "co-habitating" couple. However, two people who live together in the good faith belief that they are married, but are mistaken, are called "putative spouses." They have always had about the same rights as legally married couples. And the same is true of so-called "common law" marriages, where two people who live together for a specific period set by law regard themselves as man and wife.

Reasons for Living Together

Men and women choose to live together for a wide variety of reasons. Some, though they are lovers, are more room-mates than couples. Others make emotional and financial commitments to one another that are stronger than the commitments of marriage. And others see living together as a trial marriage of sorts.

The expectations of persons living together vary just as widely. Consider the following four examples:

John and Karen are college students who plan to live together for the rest of the school year and then go their separate ways.

Dan and Linda both work and agreed to share expenses as well as housekeeping equally. Dan pays for their vacations and Linda keeps the apartment clean. Maybe they'll get married if things work out.

Bob and Maria have lived together for the last eight years and see no reason to change this arrangement. Their salaries are equally high, and they generally pool their money. They share a house, a son, a rental unit, and a bassett hound.

Al and Diane, two retirees in their late sixties, moved in together after discovering that marriage would reduce their social security and pension income.

All four of these couples are unmarried men and women who share housing and the same bed. But that is *all* they have in common. Each of these couples expects very different things from living together; they handle their finances differently; and they probably have different commitments to each other.

To complicate the picture further, each of these couples may be in one of the following categories (depending on their particular circumstances):

- those who have made a non-marital agreement and live in a so-called "Marvin" state
- those who have not made an agreement but live in a "Marvin" state
- those who have made an agreement and do not live in a "Marvin" state
- those who have not made an agreement and do not live in a "Marvin" state

(A "Marvin" state refers to those states following the rules established in the *Marvin vs. Marvin* case, which is discussed later.)

Is Living Together Legal?

This is not as ridiculous a question as it might sound, despite the widespread change in attitude these days. In some states, living together with a person of the opposite sex outside the marriage relationship is still technically illegal.

Only about half the states have legalized all private sex acts between consenting adults. Less than half prohibit cohabitation, living together, and fewer still outlaw fornication — voluntary sexual intercourse with a person of the opposite sex.

Generally, though, our sex laws are being liberalized. Even where anti-cohabitation and anti-fornication laws remain on the books, these laws are seldom enforced. Living together or not, adults who engage in garden-variety heterosexual sex in the privacy of their homes are unlikely to be prosecuted criminally.

Common Law Marriage Common law marriage is largely an institution of the past, but some states still provide that

31

when two people act as if they are married, inten⌐ to be married, and hold themselves out to the public as being married, then they are legally married. This is called "common law marriage."

Couples married in this manner have the same legal status and the same rights and duties toward each other as other married couples. The domestic relations laws and inheritance laws of the states recognizing common law marriage consider them to be married. Couples who have established a common law marriage have no need for a non-marital agreement. And, like other marriages, common law marriage ends only by divorce or death.

Common law marriages are valid in the following states:

Alabama	Iowa	Oklahoma
Colorado	Kansas	Pennsylvania
District of	Montana	Rhode Island
Columbia	New Hampshire*	South Carolina
Georgia	Ohio	Texas
Idaho		

Suppose you live in a state that still recognizes common law marriage and you move in with a woman. Under the common law rule, are you married? Not necessarily. You must *intend* to be married to her, and intent is shown by actions.

For example, if you introduce a woman as your wife to everyone you know, and then live with her as your wife for a period of time, this might be interpreted as showing your intent to be married. Unfortunately, whether you have a valid common law marriage or not is decided by the courts only *after* you have a problem. Therefore, we suggest that in order to protect yourself and the woman you live with, if you want to be married you go through a ceremony, and if you want to be single don't act as though you're married!

Note: States that do not recognize common law marriages will accept the valid common law marriage of another state. For example, if you had a valid common law marriage in

---

*Recognized only for limited inheritance purposes.

Ohio but have moved to New York, New York will also consider you married.

Putative Spouses

Rachael married George 18 years ago and mistakenly believed that her divorce from a former marriage was final. It was not. George died last year, and his heirs are attempting to show that as Rachael's marriage was not legally valid, she has no claim to George's estate.

George's heirs are mistaken; Rachael has a valid claim to George's estate. Occasionally two people get married in good faith, both believing the marriage is legal, but for some reason or other it is not legal. Technically, of course, they are unmarried. The law, however, treats them as though they were married, and generally they have all the rights and duties of married people. As is true with common law partners, no agreement is necessary or even very relevant.

Traditional States — Property Rights on Separation

First, agreements between two adults (whether married or not) are usually valid and enforceable *anywhere* if the agreement concerns real or personal property or the payment of money for services rendered. The only problem in any state is if the agreement's chief purpose is to provide a legal framework for living together without being married. If this *is* the purpose of the agreement, a few states refuse to enforce *any* mutual agreement made by the couple, regardless of what it deals with.

If You Have No Agreement   The courts in most states have developed various methods to determine the property rights of unmarried couples who are separating. Generally, if the partners have no agreement covering their respective interests, the courts rule that money belongs to the person who earns it and that property belongs to the person who owns it (the person in whose name it stands).

33

There are exceptions, of course, where fairness dictates that a different rule be applied. For example, an unmarried person might permit his or her partner to manage all the money and property they acquire jointly, and that partner may buy property in his or her name only. In such a situation, the courts will try to equalize matters by applying legal theories such as resulting trusts and constructive trusts that mean little to the lay person.

Confusion in the Law   No state legislature has taken on the unpopular task of establishing a set of rules for property distribution when unmarried couples separate. And this probably also is an impossible task. What set of rules could apply both to a couple who equally share living expenses for two months and another couple who live together for forty years?

This has forced the *courts* to make the law for unmarried couples. The result is an inconsistent and confused legal situation. The decisions of some courts apply only to a specific couple, others to all unmarried couples in a state. To further confuse the issue, courts in some states make very different decisions with basically the same set of facts.

Unfortunately, this leaves unmarried couples unsure exactly as to what set of rules will apply in a given situation and state. However, since living together has become more commonplace, the law is changing rapidly, and courts are setting standardized rules for the various states. The *Marvin* case in California is an example of this.

Some states have had the *Marvin* legal issues presented to them directly, while others have not as yet. Of those that have decided expressly whether to follow *Marvin* or not, our research shows the following:

States Accepting Marvin:

California	Illinois	New Jersey
Oregon	Minnesota	New York

States Rejecting Marvin:

Nevada	Washington

Undecided:

Massachusetts

The following is a list of states which, to our knowledge, have not yet been presented with the issue but whose past legal history makes it unlikely they will accept the *Marvin* case:

Arizona	Kentucky	Pennsylvania
Arkansas	Louisiana	Vermont
Florida	Maine	Wisconsin
Georgia	Ohio	Wyoming
Iowa	Oklahoma	

Important Caution: The law in this area is *court law* and changes so rapidly that each reader should check for himself or herself to verify the above lists at any given time.

However, if you are an unmarried couple in a state that doesn't follow the *Marvin* case and are living together without an agreement, you're taking your chances and should be extremely careful about separating your property and keeping it separate. You may not get much help from the judge.

If You Have an Agreement As mentioned earlier, there are a few states that will not honor or enforce any agreement between an unmarried couple, whether it has to do with the relationship or with buying a house. These states feel that honoring non-marital contracts will encourage the use of them and promote the habit of living together.

In most states, though, if an agreement applies to property of any kind (land, money, stocks, furniture, and so on) the agreement is enforceable. Some states have enforced agreements between unmarried couples by separating the property part of the agreement from the living-together part of it. In short, the courts in these states ignore the part of the agreement in which the promises of living together are made.

If you live in a state that has not as yet expressly recognized living-together agreements, go ahead and make your agreement as to each person's money and property rights. Make sure, however, that the terms of your agreement do *not* depend on one of you doing something that cannot be measured in money. For example:

Don promises to pay all expenses if Jane lives with him.

This type of agreement will be *void* in these states. However, if part of the agreement reads as follows, the chances are good that the courts will enforce it:

Don promises to pay all expenses, and Jane promises to clean and maintain the home.

Marvin vs. Marvin — What Does It Mean?

In October 1964, Michelle Triola and Lee Marvin began living together. Like many couples, these two entertainers made some promises to each other. Also like many couples, years later each had a different recollection of their original promises. Michelle's story is that Lee promised to take care of her for life if she gave up her career and became his companion and helpmate. Lee thinks that he only agreed to pick up the tab for Michelle's expenses while they were living together.

During their six years together, Lee became rich and Michelle's career withered away to just about nothing. The two never married, although Michelle did change her last name to Marvin. In 1970, when they split up, Lee continued to support Michelle. A year later the checks stopped coming, and Michelle sued Lee for half the money he had accumulated during the time they had lived together (which would have been called community property if they had been married).

First, the trial court decided that as Michelle and Lee had never married, she had no right to sue him. Michelle believed that she did have the right and appealed. The California Supreme Court agreed with her and sent the case back to court for trial. In the end, Michelle was awarded $104,000 for the purposes of her "rehabilitation."

Contracts — Written or Verbal *Marvin vs. Marvin* was a California decision, and the law described in this section is primarily California law. However, *Marvin* seems to have been the first in a series of similar court decisions nationwide.

The personalities involved in this case and the sensational publicity it received are not very important in the long run.

A bitter couple broke up, and a very rich man was forced to pay his discarded female companion an amount of money he could obviously afford.

However, the case of *Marvin vs. Marvin* is very important from a legal standpoint. The case established the power of unmarried couples to make written, verbal, or implied contracts between themselves, as long as the agreements are not based on sex.

Sarah and Juan live together, and Sarah agrees to compensate Juan for doing all the housekeeping chores. This is a valid agreement. On the other hand, if Sarah agreed to pay Juan for sleeping with her, their agreement would not be valid.

Admittedly, people who live together and care for each other, married or not, seldom have neatly separated financial arrangements, nor should they, necessarily. You may support your partner after she loses her job, or she may quit her job after you are transferred to another community. These matters probably make little difference as long as you stay together, but should you separate, both of you may be confused and fight about who owns and owes what. Under *Marvin*, an agreement in lieu of marriage will provide you both, as well as the court, with the rules for settling your joint affairs.

Marvin also gives you the option of being flexible in your financial arrangements. Married couples do not have this privilege — their financial affairs must follow the domestic relations law of their state. *Marvin* specifically exempts unmarried couples from domestic relations law. For example, a married man has a duty to support his wife, but an unmarried man who makes a contract with his partner can choose whether or not to obligate himself to her and to what extent.

Implied Contracts — Quantum Meruit
So far, *Marvin* seems simple and fair. However, the California court did not stop here. It ventured into some sticky and ambiguous territory when it added the following statement:

In the absence of an express contract, the courts should inquire into the conduct of the parties to determine whether that conduct

demonstrates an implied contract, agreement of partnership or joint
venture, or some other tacit understanding between the parties.
The courts may employ the doctrine of quantum meruit, *equitable*
remedies such as constructive or resulting trusts, when warranted
by the facts of a case.

[Marvin vs. Marvin, 557 P2d 106, 1976]

At this point, when the court begins to deal with couples who have not made agreements of their own, it becomes harder to make sense out of *Marvin.*

Suppose that you have not made an agreement and are separating from the woman you live with. Or, suppose you want to be convinced that making an agreement with your partner is worth the time and the trouble. Here's how the courts in the states following *Marvin* will attempt to settle your financial affairs if you don't have an agreement.

The courts will first look for an *implied* contract or partnership. Yes, you can have a contract or a partnership without ever making a written or verbal agreement and even without your knowing it. The judge will examine the facts of your conduct to see if this implied contract exists. For example:

Sonja inherits a piece of land and then asks Tim, the man she lives
with, to build a cottage on the property. Nothing is written and no more
is said, but Sonja sees her new home being built. If asked, the court
will probably decide that a contract has been implied and Tim is
entitled to some compensation for his efforts.

When unable to find even an implied contract, courts can resort to the legal theories of *quantum meruit* and equitable remedies. *Quantum meruit* sounds formidable. It isn't. It simply means that a person who renders a service is entitled to fair compensation; otherwise, the person receiving the service would be "unjustly enriched." In other words, *quantum meruit* is a legal fiction designed to prevent unfairness when the courts cannot find an implied contract.

In order to apply this legal theory, the courts will examine the facts of your economic relationship and decide what is fair — whether you agreed to be fair or not. In fact, the *Marvin* case was based on the presumption that unmarried couples who live together intend to deal fairly with one another. (How would you feel offering evidence to the contrary?) *Marvin* specifically held that the person taking care of the home "can collect for the reasonable value of household services rendered, less the reasonable value of support received." [557 P2d 106]

Consider the following example:

Ralph is laid off work and, to fill his time, remodels the house of Ethel, the woman he lives with. In the meantime, Ethel's three kids move in, Ralph starts caring for them, and Ethel foots the bill for the five of them. This arrangement continues for three years until Ralph and Ethel separate. Ralph may be entitled to receive compensation for his services as homemaker and housebuilder.

Constructive and Resulting Trusts And this leaves the final *Marvin* catch-all: "equitable remedies of constructive and resulting trusts." These are reserved for situations in which fairness demands that someone be compensated.

Of course, all of these rather esoteric-sounding remedies must be proven in court before either you or your ex-roommate can collect a dime. The trial court judge will sift through the facts of your situation and then apply *Marvin* law. As this law is still relatively new, few guidelines for making decisions have been set. Furthermore, *Marvin* has not yet definitely become the law even in a majority of states. So, whatever happens in your case will largely be dependent on the judgment of the trial judge.

Remember, you may be able to avoid the ambiguity and problems of *Marvin* simply by taking advantage of your ability to make a contract with the woman you live with. The trial courts of most states will prefer to interpret your agreement rather than to probe the recesses of legal theories.

Living-Together Contracts

The contracts made by unmarried couples living together are called *living-together contracts, living-together agreements, contracts in lieu of marriage,* or simply contracts. In states following *Marvin,* contracts between unmarried couples are no different from any other contract.

Contracts are commonplace and part of our everyday lives.

A contract is simply an exchange of promises between two or more people in which each person gives up or does something of value in return for receiving something of value. Most contracts then set up rules or procedures for accomplishing this. All varieties of tangible things, acts, and services can be exchanged in contracts, including money, land, debts, service, and the like, down to the most trivial item.

Valid contracts can be interpreted and enforced by the courts, if necessary. Written, verbal, and implied contracts are all equally valid. However, a written contract is obviously preferable since it spells out the terms of the agreement and is also proof that the agreement was made. Contracts are generally valid if they are not grossly unfair to one of the parties, are not based on fraud, and do not include provisions contrary to law.

Frequently, even well-intentioned people cannot or will not follow through on the agreements they have made. Often people are unable to agree on exactly what their contract requires them to do. The courts will first interpret a contract and then order that the agreement be kept or, if this is not possible, order that the person who suffers a loss be compensated.

When Do You Need One?   Our advice: Always. But we don't expect you to follow this advice. And you are unlikely to experience any difficulties if you are living with a woman on a short-term basis and if you are not pooling your money. However, if any of the following are true for yourself or for the woman you live with, take our suggestion seriously.

• You have children, either yours jointly or from another relationship.
• Your incomes are very different or both high.
• You have savings, property, or debts that are extensive or much greater than the other person's.
• You receive public assistance.
• You pool your incomes.
• You own something of value together.
• You are engaged in a joint business venture.
• You have lived together for a long period of time.

• You contribute economically in a non-monetary way —
as a homemaker, for example.

A living-together contract is a fashionable but extremely
practical way to work out the financial obligations that you
and your partner have toward each other. Such an agreement
can provide a structure for the maintenance of your household, give each of you the security of knowing where you
stand financially, and provide a fair basis for your separation, should that be necessary. And this goes a long way
toward making a relationship easier. Such a contract won't,
of course, guarantee that your partner will continue loving
you. But then, what will?

Drawing Up Your Contract   Your contract can and should
be tailored to the way you and your partner want to live.
Flexibility is the name of the game. You may want to share
all your money or none of it. You will be able to provide for
just about any financial arrangement you wish, as long as you
are honest with each other, don't include provisions that are
against the law (make no mention of sex within the contract),
and are basically fair with each other.

Of course, writing a contract will mean that you and your
partner must talk about your relationship — what your
expectations are and what your commitment to each other is.
Obviously, this is a difficult task and forces both of you to
acknowledge that your relationship may not last forever and
that each of you is concerned with your *own* welfare and
self-interest.

You may need the help of an attorney. In order to be fair
to each other, you'll need to know what the general law is in
your state. This is particularly important if you have a great
deal of property or income. An attorney can provide you
with this information. Furthermore, he or she should be able
to tell you how the courts in your state are currently handling
contracts between unmarried people who live together. Use
your attorney only as a resource to get information and to
check over the agreement that you make yourselves. In this
way you can avoid great and usually unnecessary expenses.
If the agreement is simple, dispense with an attorney
entirely.

Mechanics   Your agreement should be in writing and in plain English. It can be short and general, or as long and detailed as you wish. However, don't burden yourselves with so many details that the contract is impossible to follow on a practical basis.

Once you make your contract, you should both sign it, date it, have it notarized, and each keep a copy.

Make a list of what each of you own (assets and debts). Generally, whatever each of you brings to the relationship should remain as your separate property. Attach this list to your contract and remember to update the list whenever necessary.

What Should the Contract Include?   Again, each agreement should be tailored to suit the individual needs of you and your partner. A format for non-marital agreements is not included in this book. Such a form would not be useful "as is" and might mislead you into assuming that the form satisfies your state's requirements as regards contracts.

However, a checklist of matters to be considered when drafting these agreements follows. Some of these items may not apply to you, and you should bear in mind that this is not an exhaustive list.

Introductory
- where appropriate, a statement that the partners have been living together since a given date and intend to so continue
- a statement of intention of agreement — to define respective property rights and to supersede (make ineffective) any rights either partner may have under *Marvin vs. Marvin*
- a recital that each person is unmarried, where appropriate, and resides in the state
- a recital of the occupation of each partner
- provision for payment of costs and attorney's fees in connection with the agreement

Duration of Agreement
- how long the agreement is to run — for a specific number of years or until a condition is fulfilled (such as one partner finishing school)

Property (refer, if you wish, to the inventory)
- an itemization of the separate property that each partner brings to the relationship
- an itemization of any joint property the partners acquired after the relationship began
- a statement, if one or both partners wish, that specific separate property is given to the partnership (to become joint property)
- a statement as to what will happen to any separate property that each of you may acquire in the future (such as by inheritance)

Important Note: If the agreement provides for the transfer of property upon the death of either of you, it must comply with the requirements of the law in your state (the Wills Act). You'll need an attorney to explain this.

Income
- the management and disposition of the income each of you earns
- the disposition of income received by either of you from sources other than work (dividends, insurance, pensions, and the like — this is separate property in most instances)

Expenses and Debts
- itemization of the separate debts each partner owes, such as prior spousal or child support
- itemization of the debts the partnership jointly owes
- provision for payment of debts
- items included as living expenses
- provision for payment of expenses

Credit, Banking, and Purchases
- provision for opening credit accounts in one or both names
- allocation of responsibility for credit purchases
- a statement of agreed limits on credit accounts
- provision for banking (savings or checking accounts and so on)
- how the partnership will handle joint purchases (in one or both names) and the disposition of those purchases in the event of separation

- a statement of intentions as to purchase of medical or dental insurance and coverage included

Maintenance of Household
- responsibility for household work
- provision, where desired, limiting other persons joining the household

Children
- the expectations of both regarding children
- an agreement on birth control or abortion (the latter is not enforceable in court)
- provision for custody and support of children during partnership and after separation
- an agreement as to what last name children will use
- an agreement on how the children are to be raised (religion, education, and so on)
- allocation of child-care responsibilities
- an agreement, where appropriate, on the adoption of children

Changing the Contract: Disagreements
- a review, at a specific period, of the contract and the procedure for changing the terms
- the procedure for resolving disagreements (such as seeking professional help, arbitration, and the like)

Ending the Contract
- provision defining what constitutes a breach of agreement
- specified damages for breach of agreement, where appropriate
- division of all property and debts
- provision for support of partner
- effect of death of one person on agreement
- signatures, date of agreement, and notarization

Non-Monetary Contributions   A contract will be especially important when one of you gives up something or does something for the relationship that cannot be given a dollars-and-cents value. Examples of this are caring for the home and the children, supporting a partner while he or she finishes going to school, or leaving a job when a partner is transferred to another area. Without a contract, it would be difficult for either of you to be compensated for such contributions as these. Neither of you would make such a substantial investment of your life and efforts to a stranger without some protection. And it is ridiculous to expect, just because you live together, that you are not entitled to the same protection.

Note: The non-monetary contribution must *not* be that of sleeping with the other person, no matter what state you live in. And in states not following the *Marvin* case, it is particularly important that the contribution be spelled out in terms of personal services for which compensation normally would be made.

Changing the Contract Your contract can be changed by mutual agreement. When you make a major purchase such as an automobile or a home, or when either of you change the way you financially contribute to the relationship, it should be put into writing. This can be done either by making a new agreement or by acknowledging in writing a new provision in your agreement.

Handling Money, Property, and Credit

Our advice to you: Keep your money, property, and credit separate. This way it is clearer what each of you owns, and that each of you is meeting your financial obligation toward the other. This does not mean that in a general way you cannot pool your incomes and expenses, or that you should always split the dinner tab down the middle. Usually, though, it is simpler to clearly divide up financial responsibilities and keep your property separate.

There is nothing to prevent you, however, from having all your money, credit, savings, and property in both of your names. This is likely to give the other person an equal right to use your property and will obligate you for the other person's debts. If that's what you intend, fine. But don't just drift into such an arrangement.

You may want or need to make major purchases together — a house, for example. In these situations, it is extremely important to state clearly and in writing how you will share ownership, how you will pay for your purchase, what will happen if one of you cannot meet your obligation, and what will happen should you separate.

How Are Benefits Affected?

Social Security The amount of social security you or your partner receives will not be affected by your living together. Since marriage may reduce benefits, retirees often choose to live together rather than to marry. In fact, before January 1979, a widow or widower who received social security retirement benefits based on the earnings of a former spouse lost his or her benefits upon remarriage. Although this problem has now been corrected, the Social Security Administration still pays married couples *less* than they would receive if they were single and receiving individual retirement benefits.

Retirees are not the only ones who choose to live together rather than to marry in order to keep their social security benefits. Many people under the age of 22 are entitled to social security because they are the dependents of deceased, disabled, or retired wage earners. When they marry, they stop being dependents and lose their benefits. For example:

Patrick's father died several years ago. Since Patrick, aged 20, is a full-time student, he is entitled to receive social security survivorship benefits for another two years. He and the woman he lives with will postpone their marriage so that Patrick can continue to receive social security income.

Welfare These benefits are also affected by living arrangements. Recipients are required by law to report their arrangements, including the names and relationships of the other people in their households. This is unlikely to be much of a problem if both of your are poor. But when one of you has a good or even moderate income, the benefit may be lost by living together.

How much is lost often depends only on your ingenuity and your understanding of the regulations. You should set up your financial agreement to meet the demands of the programs. Whenever possible, money, bills, and debts should be kept separate. A living-together contract is a good tool for doing this.

Aid to Families with Dependent Children   AFDC is intended to support needy children and their caretakers (most often parents). Medical care usually comes with AFDC.
Sally and her two children are supported solely by AFDC. She meets Jerry, and electrician who earns $2,000 a month. They decide to live together, and Sally and her family move into Jerry's home.

Will Sally lose some or all of her AFDC? The answer is: It depends. AFDC regulations do not prevent Sally from living with Jerry. The regulations do require that Jerry support himself, which he obviously does quite well. The regulations also state that anything Jerry gives Sally over his share of the expenses is income to Sally. This income will reduce Sally's check. Income can be free housing and food, as well as money.

A bit of financial rearrangement may keep Sally's checks coming. Jerry can pay Sally a certain amount each month to cover his expenses (the minimum required by his state). Sally can pay Jerry rent, which is, coincidentally, exactly that portion of her welfare grant allotted to housing costs. This will probably result in a minimum reduction in her income. The important principle for them to remember is to keep their financial arrangements separate and business-like — on the surface, at least.

Supplemental Security Insurance   SSI is paid by the state and federal governments to needy aged and disabled persons. Whatever income a person has, including free housing and food, is deducted from the monthly check. If you or your partner receive SSI, you would be wise to keep your money separate and not provide the receiving person with reportable income.

Food Stamps   Food stamps are given to low income *households*. When you cook together, share food, and eat meals together, you are a food stamp household, and the incomes of both of you will be considered to determine if you are both eligible. This means that you and your partner must both be poor in order for you to get food stamps. If only one of you is, this person must make a convincing argument that he or she buys, cooks, and eats food separately.

Insurance, Pension, and Fringe Benefits   Part of the income of almost all salaried people consists of fringe benefits. These may include medical and dental insurance plans, pension rights, disability benefits, and so on. In most instances, private or public (civil service) employers include coverage for the employee's dependents at a reduced charge or at no charge.

Normally, if your wife works, you receive these benefits through her employment and she through yours. People who live together generally receive none of these benefits, since in almost all instances "dependents" are defined as one's spouse or children.

There are questions, however, as to exactly how the law will treat unmarried persons' rights in regard to some of these benefits.

In addition to exclusion from social security benefits, as mentioned earlier, some of the benefits you will *not* receive through your unmarried working partner are:
- Medicare or Medicaid coverage
- company pension or annuity rights
- medical or dental insurance
- credit union access
- life insurance
- disability benefits
- worker's compensation coverage

Children and Previous Support Obligations

From Previous Relationships   Any spousal or child support that you or your partner may be obligated to pay from a former relationship is *not* affected by your living-together arrangement. Your previous family debts have legal priority over any obligations you may incur in the new relationship. However, if you happen to be living with a wealthy woman, your prior obligations will not be increased because of your good fortune.

Child support payments that are *received* by either you or your partner should not be affected by your unmarried status. However, if you or your partner receive spousal support from a prior relationship, some states will automatically terminate the obligation. Others may reduce it on the basis that your circumstances have changed.

In the Present Relationship   The rights of unmarried fathers toward their children are expanding and, in many states, are equal to those of married fathers. Furthermore, the legal distinctions between legitimate and illegitimate children are becoming a thing of the past.

However, it is important that you take several steps in order to protect your child and yourself. You and your child's mother should both acknowledge in writing that you are your child's father. (For a general format, see Chapter Four.) Then, of course, you are equally responsible for the support and care of the child. In most states, while you live together and as long as there is no court order specifying differently, both you and your child's mother will have joint custody of your child.

Inheritance laws vary from state to state. Most states do not discriminate against illegitimate children in matters of inheritance. However, if you wish your child to inherit from you, it is safer to make a will.

Obligations to Your Partner's Children   If your living-together agreement provides for support of your partner's children by a former relationship, the agreement, of course, controls the situation.

In the absence of any agreement, you have no responsibility for such children, nor does she for your children. Anything each of you do in this regard is voluntary.

But, as usual, there is a catch. If you do support your partner's children and treat them as your own for a good period of time, you may incur continuing obligations to them. Fortunately, there is a way out of this predicament, if you wish, short of committing yourself for life or depriving children you really care about. This solution is to make, as part of your agreement, a provision that you will support the children in return for their mother's performance of essential services (such as housekeeping and child-care). Alternatively, you can both agree that you will incur no obligation whatever, despite the circumstances.

Tax Considerations

You may cut your tax bill by living together rather than marrying or you may not — it depends. More than 40 tax laws turn on marital status.

Couples whose incomes are moderate-to-high and are relatively equal usually pay less income tax if they are unmarried. However, if your respective incomes differ significantly, you will probably pay less tax if you are married. This is particularly true if the person with the lower income has dependents.

The potential tax savings of an unmarried couple, however, may be offset by the loss of tax advantages available during the marriage or upon divorce following the death of one of the spouses.

Unanswered Questions for Unmarried Couples

Since the law governing the rights of unmarried couples is relatively new, a number of important questions will probably arise in the near future that will have to be decided by the courts. Among these are:

- Does an unmarried partner have an insurable interest in the other person's life?
- What specific effect does the misrepresentation of marital status have in insurance applications?
- Does an unmarried partner fall within policy definitions of beneficiaries in various policies (for example, automobile, medical, or homeowner's policies)?
- What liability does an unmarried partner have for the negligent acts of his or her partner?

• Can one partner be forced to testify against his or her partner contrary to the husband-wife privilege?
• Will the *Marvin* decision be extended to include obligations to a partner's children?
• Can an unmarried partner sue a third person for causing injury to or the death of his or her partner?

These questions, and others, may concern you. If so, you should seek legal help.

Ending Your Relationship

Breaking up is difficult. And feuding over property won't make you feel any better or stop the inevitable. Follow your contract, if you have one. If not, try to agree to a fair solution and be prepared to concede more than you feel is your obligation.

Couples who cannot agree may be able to go to court, but we suggest that you try counseling first. Go to court only if you believe that your financial survival depends on it. Court proceedings will be costly and time consuming. Consider Lee Marvin and Michelle Marvin: they lived together for six years and spent the following nine years in and out of court. Was Michelle's $104,000 (less attorney's fees) worth this?

Marrying the Woman You Live With

Marriage will change your legal relationship. If you had a living-together contract, this contract will no longer be valid, and your financial affairs will be governed by the domestic relations laws of your state. Since the financial rules will change after marriage, we again suggest that you take an inventory of your property before you marry and agree on what each of you owns separately and what you own jointly. This inventory will come in handy when making a premarital agreement (which is highly recommended).

Some practical reasons for marriage include tax advantages, if your incomes are not equal, and possible insurance, pension, and social security benefits. But these reasons are unlikely to have much to do with your decision. Whatever your reasons — good luck and best wishes.

4
Father and Child:
The Legal Ties

The father-child relationship is one aspect of domestic relations law in which men's rights have actually been expanded and their more burdensome obligations diminished.

This change is rooted in the expansion of women's rights and power outside of the family. Courts and legislators were confronted with mothers who were no longer financially disadvantaged and fathers who sought more immediate participation in their children's lives. They were also mandated to remove the stain of sexism and inequality from the law. When sexual discrimination was barred in education and employment, fairness dictated that it also be removed in family matters.

The result, in most states, is that family law has been de-sexed. Fathers and mothers are referred to as individuals or parents rather than as husbands and wives. More importantly, the new law equalizes the rights and duties of parents in matters relating to their children — at least on the books. There are a few exceptions that will be discussed later. (Even politicians can't completely de-sex a family.)

This change is not only fair, it is also the first practical step taken in decades by the courts and legislatures to *strengthen* family ties.

Given this secure legal basis, the father is as free as the mother to develop a parental relationship with his children according to his needs, desires, and ability. Should he separate from his child's mother, he need not necessarily separate from his child. And children now have the security of two parents, *both* of whom are resources for their support, welfare, and custody.

This sounds like a much rosier picture for all concerned. But the modern American child has a third parent — the government. The U.S. taxpayer foots the bill for countless children for whom nobody can or will assume financial responsibility. These children include those supported by welfare (AFDC) payments, those who are wards of the court, and those needing day-care centers, counseling, free lunches, Head Start programs, and the like.

As these costs increase and taxpayer anger mounts, the lawmakers have sought to shift the financial responsibility elsewhere. And elsewhere is often the most convenient man. Much of the inequality that remains in family law stems from the politicians' need to make someone other than the taxpayer responsible for these children.

The reality, then, is that men are at the head of the line when financial responsibility is the issue. But when men assert their affirmative rights to their children, they may find themselves at the end of the line. After all, equality with the child's mother is *only* the law — and then only in some states.

In practice, the priority in satisfying rights seems to be as follows: the child, the mother, the taxpayer, and then the father. But while you wait your turn, console yourself with the fact that ten years ago you might not even have had a place in this line.

Paternity: Who and What Is a Father?

This is obviously one area of family law that has not been de-sexed. Conflicts in this area relate specifically to the fact that men and women are different. As of yet no one has solved the inescapable — that the identity of a child's mother is certain and the identity of the father is not.

However, an established father-child relationship is essential to the law. In the past it was essential to social order, the preservation of the family, and the transfer of property.

Today lawmakers are probably more concerned with the realities of child support and providing the child with a stable home life.

Our legal system has chosen to resolve this dilemma by what we have termed "the most convenient man principle." Whenever possible, a child is given a father by the courts — a situation that may or may not conform to biological reality.

Natural and Legal Fathers The *natural father* is the biological father of the child. The *legal father* is that unlucky man who by legal definition is the father when in fact he is not the biological father.

Legitimacy A *legitimate child* is born to parents who are legally married to each other. An *illegitimate child* is born to parents who are not. These terms are increasingly falling into disuse and being replaced by the more neutral *marital child* and *non-marital child*.

The traditional concept of illegitimacy is becoming a thing of the past. Some states have adopted laws such as the Uniform Parentage Act and the Uniform Paternity Act, which provide legal equality for children whether their parents were married or not. Other states have enacted similar laws, and recently the United States Supreme Court has mandated that the rights of children be equalized regardless of the married status of their parents.

The Married Father In the usual situation — that of a married man whose wife has a child — the man's paternity is established by the filing of the birth certificate or by his express acknowledgment that he is the father.

Under the Uniform Parentage Act and similar laws, unless you are impotent or sterile, you are *conclusively presumed* to be the father of any children conceived by your wife while you are living with her.

"Conclusively presumed" means that you are out of luck. No matter what the realities of your situation, you will be considered the child's legal father. You cannot offer any proof to the contrary. Consider the following actual case:

In California a black child brought a paternity action against a black man, alleging that he was her father. The child's mother and her husband were white and had other white children. The husband was conclusively presumed to be the child's father.

There are some complicated exceptions to this rule that may allow a man the right to *try* to prove that he is not the father. If you are stuck with being a legal "father," you should seek the help of an attorney.

Annulled Marriage   An annulled marriage is a marriage that is legally deemed never to have existed. If you had children and your marriage was later annulled, the legitimacy of your children and your rights as their father are generally assured.

Artificial Insemination   Some states allow artificial insemination of a wife, either with the semen of her husband or that of a donor, if she is unable to bear children otherwise. She must obtain her husband's consent (in writing) before she can be artificially inseminated. This consent must be filed with the appropriate state agency, usually the State Department of Health.

The insemination procedure must be under the supervision of a licensed physician, who must certify the signatures of the husband and wife on the consent form as well as the date of insemination.

All papers and records, including the consent form, are confidential and kept in a sealed file by the state agency. They may be inspected only when it can be shown in court that there is good cause for examining them.

In states where the problem has been considered, a child by artificial insemination is treated like any other natural child. The father is treated as the natural father (even where his wife was inseminated artificially with semen donated by another man). He has the same duty of support to the child as he would to his own natural children.

The Unmarried Father   Recently the rights of unmarried fathers to their children have been expanded — from none to a few. This gain is the result of both new statutory family law and court decisions. Before the modernization of the law dealing with the rights of unmarried fathers, the unmarried mother had the sole right to the child's custody, earnings, and services. The father was required to support the child but had no rights.

The legislative trends toward establishing the legal equality of male and female parents and toward abolishing the legal classification of illegitimacy have helped the unmarried father. He now has a basis for asserting his claims to his children.

The courts are increasingly being confronted with unmarried fathers who are demanding their rights in a positive sense. These fathers do not want to contest paternity or evade the responsibilities of being a parent. They want to *establish* their rights (and duties) as their child's parent.

In one of its more famous decisions in this area, *Stanley vs. Illinois,* the United States Supreme Court recognized the parental rights of unmarried fathers. Mr. Stanley had several children by a woman with whom he had lived on and off for 18 years. The mother died, and the children became wards of the court, since Illinois law presumed unmarried fathers to be unfit parents. The Court struck down this law and gave Mr. Stanley a chance to show in Court that he was a fit parent. This case was a "first."

Ironically, the courts have had little difficulty fixing an unmarried father's responsibilities; unmarried fathers have been paying child support for hundreds of years. They must still, alas, pay for their "sins."

Establishing Paternity The legal presumptions mentioned in regard to married men do not apply to unmarried men. Other presumptions *do* apply. None, however, apply *conclusively.*

An unmarried father may establish his paternity to a child, that is, he may be legally considered the child's father. In most states, and in all states conforming to the Uniform Parentage Act, a father may "legitimate" a child and become his or her legal father by:

- marrying the child's mother either before or after the child's birth
- taking the child into his home and acknowledging the child as his own (see form below)
- bringing a paternity action in court to establish the father-child relationship

The first two ways should not require any legal help. The third obviously does.

Recently some fathers have been confronted with a situation in which they desired to establish their paternity and their child's mother denied their parentage. Consider the following example:

Sally becomes pregnant and asks Brian, the father, to do the honorable thing — to marry her. Brian indicates that his honor would be better served by not being a husband. Sally tells him he can forget being a father. When their child is born, she refuses to accept his acknowledgment of paternity and does not allow him contact with the baby.

Obviously, you can best protect your interests and those of your child by having a clear and *written* understanding with the child's mother that you are the child's father. If you can secure the mother's cooperation, we suggest that you *both* sign an acknowledgment of your parenthood. In the majority of states this will be sufficient. See Form 1. When the mother's cooperation cannot be secured we suggest that you use Form 2.

At least three copies of one of these Forms should be prepared and each copy should be notarized. One copy is for you, one for the mother, and one for the child. Be sure and check with the court or your state Bureau of Vital Statistics to see if they have a procedure for filing your statement with them.

Contesting Paternity Suppose you are a married man but the birth of your wife's child comes under one of the rare exceptions to the presumption mentioned above. Or suppose you are unmarried and want to contest a woman's claim that you are the father of her child.

The most obvious way to prove you are not the father is

by proving that you and the mother could not have had sexual relations during the time she became pregnant. (If you are impotent or sterile you may, of course, establish this and rebut her claim.)

Another method of disproving paternity allegations is by blood test evidence. This method is tricky, since a number

---

ACKNOWLEDGMENT OF PARENTHOOD

We *(name of father)* and *(name of mother)* state that we are the natural parents of *(name of child)* born _____, 19__, in *(name of city)* in the State of _____.

(Name of father) hereby acknowledges that he intends and believes that he has taken all steps necessary to fully legitimate *(name of child)* for all purposes, including, but not limited to, the right to inherit from and through him at the time of his death.

Date: _____ 19__   _____
                                        (Name of father)

                              _____
                                        (Name of mother)

Form 1.

of states have complicated rules under which this kind of evidence may or may not be allowed. Tissue samples are much more accurate and conclusive than blood samples. If you are contesting a paternity claim, we suggest you locate a laboratory that does tissue samples for this purpose. Your physician may be of help.

ACKNOWLEDGMENT OF PATERNITY

(Name of father) hereby acknowledges that he is the natural father of _(name of child)_ , born _____, 19__, to _(name of mother)_ in _(name of city)_ in the State of _____.

(Name of father) hereby acknowledges that he intends and believes that he has taken all steps necessary to fully legitimate _(name of child)_ for all purposes, including, but not limited to, the right to inherit from and through him at the time of his death.

Date: _____, 19__   _____
                                        (Name of father)

Form 2.

The court proceedings in a paternity action vary from state to state and, of course, your attorney will be in charge. Note, however, that if the judge finds that you are the father, he or she will also make orders regarding your duty of support to the child and, hopefully, visitation orders and the like.

Once Paternity Is Established   Remember, once paternity is established, you are the child's father forever. Paternity, unlike any other relationship, cannot be terminated by mutual consent. Courts are traditionally very reluctant to sever the parent-child tie. Your rights and duties to your child will end only when you voluntarily consent to another man's adoption of your child, when the court rules otherwise, or when your child comes of legal age. In fact, even adult children continue to have a legal relationship with their parents in matters of inheritance.

Adoption   The rights of unmarried fathers were recently expanded in regard to adoption of their children without the fathers' consent. In New York state, an unmarried mother commenced an adoption of her child without first obtaining the father's consent. This was proper under New York law.

The father's objections were finally ruled on by the United States Supreme Court. That court held, for the first time, that an unmarried father may contest adoption proceedings involving his child where he has not consented. This is a landmark case for unmarried fathers.

The Duties of Child Support

Traditionally the father has been the chief parent charged with the duty to support minor children. Until fairly recently most states had a law like the following:

Every man shall support his wife and child when in need . . .
[Former Cal Civ C § 242]

Over thirty-five states have amended these laws to:

Every individual shall support his or her spouse and child when in need . . .
[Cal Civ C § 242]

As stated previously, the duty of an unmarried father to support his child is a time-honored tradition. Only his rights as a father are a revolutionary concept.

It is chiefly the taxpayer and the child's mother who demand payment of child support, and often they will assume that a father's major interest is to avoid paying child support. Although the child's mother also has, and always has had, a duty to support the child, this duty is seldom enforced. The father's duty, assuming his availability, is always enforced. This means that the unmarried father can expect to find himself grouped with married fathers when the bills come due.

Generally all the following material applies equally to both unmarried and married fathers. "Mother" or "unmarried partner" may be substituted for "wife," where appropriate.

How Much Support?   You and your child's mother must provide your child with what the law calls "necessaries." These are:
   • suitable food, housing, furniture, and clothing
   • medicine and medical attention
   • means of education
   • social opportunity and protection
Each of these items is discussed in detail in Chapter Fourteen.

If you or your child's mother have the means to support your minor child but fail to, you can expect a visit from the local governmental agency charged with enforcing such laws. Note that fathers, like mothers, have the right to apply for welfare when they do not have the means to support their children.

When the Child Lives Away from Home   Generally a father (or mother) is not liable for the ordinary expenses of a minor child who lives away from home and supports himself or herself.

Jim, over his parents' protest, leaves home to live with his girlfriend. He gets a job as an apprentice machinist and does pretty well. Jim's parents are not liable for his basic support.

You may live in a state where the law exempts you from child support if your child has left your home without "justifiable cause," that is, if nothing you did caused your child to leave. But if your conduct or abandonment of the child caused him or her to leave home, you are still liable for support.

Pete's father was always drunk at home and mistreated his wife and children. Pete couldn't take it any more and went to live with a friend. Pete's father is liable for Pete's support.

Sharon's dad went to Philadelphia on a business trip and hasn't been seen for six months. The family is desperate, and Sharon takes a room-and-board job as a housekeeper. If and when they find him, Sharon's dad is liable for her support.

Regardless of what the law provides generally, if your child leaves home, gets into trouble, and is placed in some kind of institution such as a juvenile hall, you will be billed for his or her care and maintenance.

Paul, aged 16, leaves home, gets a job, an apartment, and a girlfriend. He and the girl are picked up smoking dope and detained at juvenile hall. Paul's parents will have to spring for his bill.

Stepfathers The laws of almost all states provide that an individual is not bound to support his or her spouse's children by a former relationship. But, if you take such children into your family and support them, the law presumes that you do so as a parent and in effect makes you the child's legal parent. This means that you're stuck with support unless you can prove that becoming a parent to the child was not your intention. (Another example of "the most convenient man" principle.)

The father of Harold's three stepchildren is a plain deadbeat. He's full of promises but hasn't contributed a dime in years. Harold doesn't want his stepchildren to starve. He doesn't want to divorce his wife. Nor does he want to assume permanent responsibility for his stepchildren's support.

The Harolds of this world have some avenues open to protect themselves and still see that their stepchildren are provided for. If you find yourself in a situation like this, the most obvious course is to have your wife really attempt to enforce the child support orders. If this fails, you and your wife can, in consultation with your attorney, draw up an agreement whereby the children are supported and their stepfather is not permanently obligated.

Stepfathers who wish to establish their legal rights to their stepchildren should remember that support alone will not make them the child's father. The natural father's rights must be terminated by his consent or court order, and then the stepfather must adopt his stepchild.

Emancipation of Children You and your children's mother are liable for the support of your children until they reach their majority, that is, until they are of age. In some states this is at age 21, in some at 18.

When a minor child is freed from his or her legal parental ties and the child secures the rights and duties of an adult, the child is "emancipated." When this happens the parents no longer have an obligation to support the child.

Remember that when in doubt, the courts will generally obligate you to support your child. Again, better you than the taxpayer.

The marriage of the child is the most common example of emancipation. Enlistment in the military is another. And a child may be emancipated when he or she has left home and is self-supporting.

Support of Adult Children If your child is physically or mentally unable to care for himself or herself after coming of age, your responsibility as a father depends on which state you live in. Some states have laws that require a parent to support such an adult child. In other states a father has no such legal obligation unless the child was incapacitated before he or she came of age. And frequently state laws will hold a father liable for an adult child's care in a state institution.

If you are a father who has a problem involving the support and maintenance of an adult child, your best bet is to get legal advice as to the laws of your state.

Father's Rights to a Child's Property, Services and Earnings Adults, parents, and even men occasionally deserve fantasies. Here's one for you:

Bill was blessed with a very ambitious daughter. Laurie, at five, opened her first lemonade stand. By ten she had parlayed this into a health food restaurant, which quickly went national. Laurie, now 15, continues building her financial empire. Bill is diligently exercising his fatherly control while eating mangoes in Hawaii. Of course, all Laurie's profits belong to him (and his wife).

Parents have no ownership rights, as such, in their child's property. However, parents are equally entitled to a child's services (work) and earnings, and may use the earnings as they see fit. Generally a child's employer may pay the child his or her wages directly unless notified by the parents that they claim the child's wages.

In most states an unmarried mother is entitled to a child's services and earnings unless the father has become a legal father by a presumption of law. This law may change, as have other laws expanding the rights of unmarried fathers.

If you and your wife separate, the right to the child's work and earnings usually goes to the parent having custody. But the child's earnings are a factor in determining how much child support should be awarded.

Children usually only become rich if their grandfather or grandmother leaves them something. And here you are out of luck. Anything kids acquire as a gift or through inheritance is their own. As a parent you may be given the responsibility of managing their riches, but that's as close as you get.

Exceptions There are some exceptions to these rules. If your child is an actor or actress or in professional sports, the court must usually approve his or her contract. When this is the case, the judge may order you or a third person to set up a trust fund or a savings plan for the child.

Another exception is where your child receives money from a judgment he or she has recovered against someone else. The parents, as the guardians, must set up a court-approved trust fund with the proceeds. And finally, any money a minor child receives from such sources as unemployment insurance benefits is paid to the child in his or her own right.

A Father's Authority

Traditionally the father was responsible for controlling his family. He had the right and, at times, the duty to discipline his children. And his children had the duty to obey him. This concept, of course, has been watered down considerably over the years. What are we left with? A system that expects a father to control and discipline his child and expects a child to obey his father but provides few legal supports to make it happen.

So, legally what means do you have to discipline your children? Naturally you can talk to them, deprive them of weekly ice-cream cones, and restrict them from driving your car. But can you spank them, give them the strap, or beat the daylights out of them? Generally a father may physically discipline his children moderately; he may not inflict abuse on or criminally assault them.

What does "moderate" mean? "Moderate" is supposedly judged in relation to the standards of your community, which, of course, are anyone's guess. If you live in California (as we do), you'd best not bruise your child's tender rear end. In some states, authorities and judges view physical discipline as an acceptable way to control a child. In these states you may be able to reasonably spank your kid without hearing from his lawyer.

So-called experts agree, of course, that physical discipline is worse than bad — it's ineffective. Regardless of the merits of this pronouncement, this view seems to prevail. Our advice? Don't assume you can physically discipline your child the way your parents disciplined you.

Are you as a father confused as to where this leaves you? If so, consider this example from a recent court case:

A parent (a mother in this case) had reason to believe her kid was a dope dealer. When he wasn't home one day, she searched his room and found a considerable quantity of dope and paraphernalia.
An appeals court threw the case out on the ground of illegal search and seizure. The judges stated that his mother had no right to search the room without the kid's permission or a search warrant.

Now, read the following section and discover the consequence of failing to control your child.

Liability of a Father

Technically a parent is not liable for the acts of his or her child that damage other persons or property, *unless* the parent was careless and that carelessness led to the damage. You'd better not be too smug about this rule, though. Any time your child causes property or personal damage, there's an excellent chance that the person damaged can show that you, the parent, were careless.

Furthermore, a number of states have laws that hold you as a parent liable for certain damage your kid does whether you were careless or not. For example, many states hold a parent absolutely liable for the damage caused when junior gets bored and burns down the little red schoolhouse. Such laws are based on a parent's failure to control a child.

You, as a parent, are almost invariably stuck with the bill when your child is at fault in an automobile accident. Your liability is assured on two counts. First, you are probably the registered owners of the vehicle your child was driving, which makes you liable. Second, in order for your child to obtain a driver's license, you had to promise to be responsible for his or her damages. Best have a good insurance policy.

In short, you may be prevented by the law from exercising reasonable control over your child. But if you don't, you are liable for what happens. If this seems kind of *insane* to you, you don't need a shrink — just a change of legislators.

Change of Child's Last Name

In most states your child carries your surname until he or she comes of age. The father has a protectible interest in his child's family name.

There are some exceptions, such as when your child is legally adopted and you consent to a change of name. And in some instances, a child's last name may be changed by court order to avoid serious embarrassment or emotional damage to the child.

67

5
Abortion: The Silent Sire

The battle lines are clearly drawn on the moral and political issue of abortion in this country. The pro-life forces vow to uphold one of our most fundamental principles — the right of a human being to life. Those favoring abortion are equally well armed. Backed by the courts, they assert the individual's right to privacy and to control that most basic of properties — one's own body. The conflict is so intense that smart politicians and authors fear death in the crossfire.

In the heat of this battle other potentially conflicting rights have been ignored — those of the father. Even though unpopular and weakened, these rights *do* exist.

For the equality-minded woman the right to control abortion is a bottom-line, survival issue. Even the earliest feminists perceived the direct link between controlling childbearing and winning independence for women. Political and economic emancipation was an empty promise without the practical means to liberate women from the overriding demands of a house full of children.

As a result, women who are otherwise flexible and rational become stubborn and assaultive when their absolute right of choice to abortion is challenged. The mere suggestion that men may be entitled to some legal say in abortion arouses the wrath of wives, lovers, friends, daughters, and co-authors.

However, the inescapable fact is that heterosexual sex, conception, birth, and parenthood are the result of some sort of relationship between a man and a woman. A woman as an individual unquestionably should be guaranteed her rights to privacy, to control her body, and to make her own choices. But once she chooses to have a relationship, she can no longer be totally free from obligations to her partner. She cannot claim that, should she become pregnant, she is solely responsible for her condition. And she cannot claim that she is her unborn's only parent.

The law has always recognized the father's connection with his unborn child. For example, the law has unfailingly demanded that fathers maintain and support their yet-to-be-born progeny. And increasingly the courts are affirming the rights of fathers to participate in the parenting of their children. The rights of unmarried fathers have been accepted and enlarged, as have the rights of fathers generally in regard to custody of their children following divorce.

Recent changes in the law mirror the father's new image. He has again become a serious, reliable parent, although perhaps not in a traditional sense. Working mothers have demanded that men assume a share of the child-care responsibilities. Men have been subjected to the diapers but, in the process, often gained closeness with their children and self-assurance as parents. Their relationship with their children has become real and their own — not one experienced through the children's mother.

However, in 1973, when the Supreme Court legalized abortion-on-demand, it decided that a woman's right to privacy was more important than whatever rights a father had. This current abortion law does not reflect biological reality. Pregnancy is the result of a man and woman having a sexual relationship. The fetus is *their* fetus, not the woman's alone. The lives of *both* the man and the woman will be immensely affected by whatever decision is made in regard to abortion.

Furthermore, the current law reinforces very outdated and sexist stereotypes. Do "women still have most to lose by an unwanted pregnancy"? Are men "bungling parents"? Are "women always in the end responsible alone for their children"? And are "men untrustworthy in their commitments"?

70

We hesitate to suggest that the law further meddle in relationships. Obviously, decisions about abortion are best resolved by negotiation between individual men and women. But the law defines the bottom-line rights and duties in a relationship. In order for men and women to negotiate effectively, they both must feel they have some power and a stake in an equitable decision. The following proposals for changes in the abortion laws are suggested in this spirit.

Abortion: The Present Law

Years ago, when David and Janet were first married, they decided that they eventually wanted children. At 38 Janet surprisingly became pregnant. David picked up the schedule for Lamaze classes and Janet planned an abortion. David was shocked, hurt, and generally madder than hell. When his impassioned pleas didn't work, David threatened legal action. Janet told him to stop being so emotional – the abortion would go ahead as planned. It did.

Years ago, when Pete and Susan were first married, they too decided that they eventually wanted children. But they were very specific as to when — after they had both finished eight years of higher education. Five years later Susan decided babies were more interesting than books and became pregnant. Pete was furious that their agreed plans were intentionally disrupted. He asked, demanded, cajoled, pleaded, and ordered Susan to have an abortion. She refused and Pete is a father.

Under present law, established by the United States Supreme Court in 1973, David is powerless to interfere with Janet's unilateral decision to abort their child. Pete, in the second example, has no right to force Susan to have an abortion nor would he have any such right even under the old law.

In both situations at least two things are apparent: first, the pregnant woman has the power to unilaterally choose whether to terminate her pregnancy, and second, her male partner has no legal, enforceable interest in her decision. How have our laws on abortion reached these results?

Background: A Summary Before 1973, abortion was a crime unless the state approved the abortion. Approval was generally given when the pregnant woman's life or health were threatened by the birth. The criminal abortion laws reflected the long-standing moral and legal prohibitions against the taking of human life. These laws caused human suffering in many instances and were evaded when necessary by those with means. Criticism grew and pressure for legal reform mounted.

1973: Abortion Legalized By about 1970 the Women's Liberation Movement had become a social and political reality. The Movement took dead aim on the criminal abortion laws, exerting immense pressure on state and federal lawmakers to abolish these laws. The courts were also besieged by litigants and lawyers attacking the same laws. In 1973 two such cases reached the nation's highest court and made sweeping new law.

The cases were called *Roe vs. Wade* and *Doe vs. Bolton*. Both presented the abortion issue squarely. The majority of justices in both cases held that:

No state or federal laws may prohibit the taking of human fetal life in the approximate first three months (the first trimester) of its existence.

The Court further ruled that abortions may be regulated by a state during the fourth to sixth month of pregnancy but *only* to the extent of requiring safe conditions for the woman. Abortion was legalized and the law of the land was rewritten. The basis for the new law was a woman's constitutional right to privacy. This right, said the justices, was broad. Broad enough to permit a woman to terminate her pregnancy by abortion *without interference* — at least during the first trimester.

The effect of these court decisions was to invalidate state laws that made abortion a crime or required a husband's consent to the abortion. After these decisions and others like them, various state and national groups mounted political campaigns to change this court-made law. And the battle lines were drawn.

Fathers' Rights: What Are They? Before the court decisions in 1973, there was little occasion for the courts to determine what rights a father may have in his unborn child when abortion is the issue. Abortion was a crime and that was that.

After 1973, however, prospective fathers whose wives sought abortion without the father's consent looked to the courts for help. Did these fathers have any rights? What kind? How could they enforce them?

Cases by such fathers were brought before the courts in Florida, Massachusetts, Utah, Wisconsin, and New York. Some of those seeking help were unmarried and others married. Some still lived with their partners; others had separated.

In each of these cases the courts conceded that the father had rights — of some kind — in his wife's unborn child.

The father has rights. They are familial. They antedate the Constitution; they are about as old as civilization itself. They center in the main potentiality of marriage: the birth and raising of children. Few human experiences have meaning comparable to parenthood. The father's rights . . . are surely among the fundamental rights protected by the Constitution. (Hennessey, J., dissenting in Doe vs. Doe *314 NE2d 128)*

Some have called a father's rights in an unborn child "proprietary," whereas the mother's are "personal." In other words, the father's rights are similar to those he has in his property, but the mother's rights are her individual and private concern. Such stereotyping of a man and woman's interest in the birth process is badly outdated — and never was true.

It is absurd to believe that the interest of a father in his child springs into existence full grown on the day of birth. As with women, the pregnancy period is, for the father, often one of anxiety, anticipation, and growing in feeling for the unborn child. Indeed, many fathers participate during the mother's labor and delivery of the child. In short, their involvement is usually manifested upon learning of the pregnancy.

Can the Law Be Changed?

*Do not "women's rights" have to be set in the framework of the full
spectrum of human rights — species-rights, body-rights, etc. —
thus subjecting them to the possible claims of other human rights?
It is one thing to emancipate women from discrimination and male
tyranny; it is quite another to emancipate them from all human claims
and obligations toward the rights of others. But to claim or presume
an absolute right to abortion or to make "women's rights" absolute
is to create a set of rights for women subject to none of the normal
limitations of life in the human community.* *

In effect, under the present law a woman may abort her
child if she wishes. If, however, she decides to carry her child
to term, the father incurs legal liabilities for the child's care.
In neither instance does the father have an effective voice
should he disagree with the mother's decision. Is this the
kind of situation envisioned by those who support the Equal
Rights Amendment? The father's rights in his wife's ability
to have children have been recognized elsewhere. In most
states, a father may sue a person who intentionally or negli-
gently injures his wife and destroys her fetus (provided the
fetus is "viable" — about six months developed). In the
same vein, a husband may recover damages for an injury to
his wife that renders her sterile. In short, recognition of a
father's interest in the future children of his marriage is not
all that new or startling.

There simply is no way that the courts will *force* a woman
to have a child — even if they could. Still, the mother's
interest in childbearing is linked directly to her physical and
emotional wellbeing. Furthermore, if the legislature of any
state enacts a law interfering with the freedom of a woman to
have an abortion, the law will be ruled unconstitutional.

A careful reading of the opinions in the cases referred to
above gives one the impression that even the majority of
judges who reject the father's claims would *like* to accommodate those claims. But not at the expense of ordering a
woman not to have an abortion. In other words, under the

---

*Quoted with permission from *ABORTION: Law, Choice and Morality* by Daniel
Callahan (Copyright © 1970 by Daniel Callahan. Macmillan Publishing Co., Inc.,
New York.)

law as it stands the courts simply cannot solve the dilemma posed.

How Can the Law Be Changed?

We believe the law can be changed — at least to the extent that the father's interest in his unborn child is more effectively recognized and honored. Furthermore, the changes suggested do not infringe on the legal right of the mother to have her abortion under the law.

Notice to the Father At present a physician performing an abortion is under no legal obligation to notify the expectant mother's husband that she has applied for an abortion. One irony here is that physicians are "expected," though not legally required, to obtain a husband's consent to his wife's tubal ligation (sterilization).

The law can be changed to require that notice be given by physicians to husbands. Such a notice requirement before the abortion would in no way infringe on the mother's constitutional rights to have the abortion. It would, however, at least have the effect of *recognizing* the father's interest and informing him of her intentions.

What practical results would such notice achieve? First, it might provide a "cooling-off" period (a very short one), in which the woman could resolve conflicting feelings she might have about the procedure. She might reconsider her decision if it arose from a temporary problem in her relationship with her partner.

More importantly, such a requirement would expose the decision to discussion. A woman can only guess her husband's reaction before he is actually confronted with the facts. The man would be able to state his case and negotiate. And, even if he disagreed with his wife's final decision, he would gain a better understanding of his wife's feelings and of the status of their relationship. For example:

Rosalind is pregnant but determined that her successful career will not be interrupted. She applies for an abortion and her husband Sam is notified. Deeply hurt and shocked, Sam tells her the abortion

75

will end their marriage. Rosalind is angry but reflects on what divorce and the loss of her husband and home would mean to her. She and Sam talk and work out a solution whereby she can have the child, save her marriage, and still successfully pursue her career.

Another probable situation:

Kathy is pregnant and very unhappy. And telling her husband, Jason, will only mean another of their terrible fights. But their marriage is so shaky Kathy won't risk having a child. When notified, Jason is predictably furious. He just can't understand why Kathy won't settle down and act like a "normal" woman. Over his protests, Kathy has an abortion. Jason files for divorce and looks for a more accommodating partner.

Counseling   In many states when a person files for divorce each spouse must indicate whether he or she desires counseling. If either person wants this service both husband and wife must attend at least one counseling session. This procedure does not delay or stop the divorce proceedings.

Such a requirement would be very valuable in contested abortion cases such as the ones described above. Certainly this simple procedure would reflect the obvious —that a father has some moral and legal rights in his unborn child. Furthermore, such a requirement would not interfere with a woman's constitutional right to have an abortion if she wishes.

Getting Organized Politically   How can men force the law to reflect fathers' interests in unborn children and to correct the inequity of the present law? The same way women did — by being vocal about this unequal treatment, by lobbying their representatives, and by bringing cases to court. Men must convince the public and the lawmakers that fathers are serious parents and that men as well as women are irrevocably affected by the abortion decision.

Perhaps Equal Rights for Fathers might help — try them. And some women's organizations have assisted men in the enforcement of equal rights, most notably NOW (National Organization of Women). They are vocally on record as opposed to any change in the abortion law. But perhaps when women finally realize that men are equal partners in pregnancy and parenthood, their women's organizations may recognize the unfairness of the present law.

Damages for Breach of Contract

A contract is a binding agreement between at least two persons to do or not to do a certain thing. A contract creates obligations (legal duties), which may be enforced by the courts. A breach of contract is an unjustified failure by one of the parties to the contract to perform or fulfill his or her legal obligations or duties under the contract.

When one person breaches a contract the other person is legally injured and has two court remedies. First he or she can ask the court to order that the contract be performed (called "specific performance"). For example, a court can force a person to sell property if he or she has agreed to sell it under a contract. If this is not appropriate or simply can't be done, then the injured person can ask the court to award him or her damages as compensation for the breach. Damages are usually a certain amount of money.

In Traditional Marriages

Charlie and Virginia marry. Later they discuss children, and both agree that a family is essential to their future happiness. Virginia becomes pregnant but plans an abortion over Charlie's protests. When they separate, Charlie sues Virginia for breach of contract in failing to carry the child to term.

Charlie has wasted his time and money. The modern marriage "contract" does not state the rights and duties that spouses have to each other. At the altar Charlie and his bride promised only to love, honor, and cherish each other. Whatever else they must do is left for them to work out or to be decided legally when their marriage fails. Even having children, though expected, is not a right that Charlie (or Virginia) can demand because they are married.

Charlie's only recourses are to accept Virginia's decision or to divorce her and try to find a more understanding woman.

In Marriage or Partnership by Contract A judge in one of the contested abortion cases mentioned above commented: "Some things must be left to private agreement."

The judge was probably stating the obvious — that a father and mother should agree on whether to abort their child. But the language is interesting.

More and more unmarried couples live together. Some of them work out the details as they go and encounter many of the same problems that married couples do. To avoid some of the legal difficulties presented by living-together arrangements, we suggest written agreements that specify the rights and duties of each partner. Such agreements are discussed in detail in Chapter Three.

These agreements or contracts commonly state whether the partners intend to have or to adopt children. Few, however, state the intentions of the parties as to abortion (except perhaps to provide for the costs of abortion).

If the agreement expressly prohibits abortion except where the life or health of the mother is at stake, and she breaches the agreement, the courts might consider the father's lawsuit for breach of contract.

Again, the courts will not — and cannot — require the mother to perform her part of the agreement, that is, carry the baby to term. But the courts may decide that under these circumstances the father should be awarded money damages for the mother's failure to follow through on her agreement.

What would a father's damages be if he won such a lawsuit? Obviously, the worth of children to their parents cannot be measured in money. However, courts regularly award money damages for such reasons as pain, suffering, and emotional distress. The same is true for the loss of a spouse's ability to function sexually and the loss of an unborn child — none of which can be truly compensated for monetarily.

More importantly, the possibility of such a lawsuit might deter some women from obtaining abortions with *no* consideration of the father's rights. Another result might be that the partners would negotiate something that would work for both of them.

If you are an expectant father whose partner plans an abortion against your wishes and against the terms of the agreement under which you formed your partnership, call your lawyer and give it a try. Remember, new law is made from new cases — as women have learned.

No Abortion: Your Partner's Right

As mentioned above, a woman cannot be forced to have an abortion by you, by the terms of a written agreement, or by a court. The law has not changed in that respect. This is true even though the woman signed a written agreement with you that she would practice strict birth control, since neither of you wanted children.

One reason for this, obviously, is that birth control is not fail-safe. Another is that it takes two to tango. And finally, of course, no one can force a woman to undergo such a medical procedure without her consent.

If your partner becomes pregnant despite your mutual plans and agreement and decides to carry the baby to term you can either divorce your spouse, provided you live in a no-fault state; or you can decide it may be a blessing in disguise and enjoy it. You may as well try the latter — you'll have to support the baby anyway.

6
Reverse Sex Discrimination: Employment

The unfair treatment of women in the job market in the past is a historical fact and a part of the national consciousness. And some employers still practice discrimination when they can get away with it.

But things have changed. Various civil rights laws were enacted and then taken seriously. Also, conscience demanded that women be given more than just equality; they needed rapid access to jobs, promotions, and power. Accordingly, voluntary or government-mandated preferential programs such as Affirmative Action were born.

Meanwhile, back at the ranch, men were doing what came naturally — milling about like nervous cattle, talking to themselves and each other angrily, then stomping up the dust again. The clever ones left, joined the women's march incognito, grabbed the nearest "Down with Male Exploitation" sign, and marched quietly.

Today, various state and federal bureaucratic agencies are mandated to eliminate sexual discrimination in employment. These agencies are often staffed by humorless, self-righteous individuals who view equal rights as a one-way street — for women. This chapter is intended to help men realize that equality should and can work for them — if they know how to play the game.

What Is the Law?

Federal and state law prohibits discrimination in employment based on sex. These laws apply to hiring, promotions, firing, salaries, fringe benefits, and other privileges.

Reverse Discrimination Reverse discrimination (sometimes called "majority" discrimination) is a policy or practice that favors women or minority groups and discriminates against members of the "majority."

Bill, a star graduate of the local law school, has his heart set on joining a prestigious law firm. His classmate, Ellen, is competent but definitely not the cream. The firm wants to be "with it" and decides to hire a woman. Ellen is hired. And Bill is heartbroken.

The Equal Opportunity in Employment laws are clear. They do not authorize this sort of reverse discrimination — any more than they authorize discrimination against women. This, however, is only the main body and the promise of the law. As usual, the fine print reads differently. The reverse discrimination practiced widely today does have a "legal" basis. And, while most pervasive in employment, reverse discrimination casts its ugly shadow in higher education, the awarding of government contracts and loans, and other parts of the economic sector.

When the legislators, courts, and regulators were outlawing traditional sex discrimination, they were busily creating a new brand. Women had joined forces with minorities groups, and they proved to have irresistible power. The pressure they mustered created the maze of regulations, programs, and procedures that now form the basis for "legal" reverse discrimination. Employers were put in an impossible bind. They were forbidden by law to discriminate on the basis of sex (or race) but were required by "legal" guidelines and policies to hire and promote more women and minorities.

They responded to this challenge by exploiting the linguistic skills of their personnel officers. Someone clever enough with words could get around the letter of the law.

Women, minorities, and plain poor folk were transformed into "the ethnically, culturally, and economically disadvantaged." Quotas for women became "guidelines," and "An Equal Opportunity Employer" came to mean "Women and Minorities Wanted." When a female lawyer was wanted, a a job announcement specifying, "Attorney, Women's Problem Specialist" could be written. Such euphemisms for reverse discrimination usually passed the legal tests. Such practices were especially pervasive in local and federal civil service employment.

The recruitment and promotion of women went full steam ahead. Many employers hired women and hoped that they were, or could be made, competent. The bright, well-prepared woman jobseeker often was a jewel employers fought over.

Criticism of this system is surprisingly mild. Most men are fearful of attacking reverse discrimination. Fighting preferential treatment of women means not only pitting oneself against women, employers, and an entrenched bureaucracy, but also against all those with a vested interest in reverse discrimination. This odd collection of "minorities" includes, in addition to women, blacks, Hispanics, Asians, Native Americans, non-English speakers, the aged, the handicapped, ex-prisoners, junkies, and ex-mental patients. It also constitutes a large part of the U.S. population.

The courts have been employed to both challenge and support reverse discrimination. Their decisions have been consistently unclear and indecisive; they are only definitive in their dislike for the entire issue. They have ruled against preferential quotas for the disadvantaged and then ordered quotas when patterns of discrimination have been revealed.

The advocates of reverse discrimination on the basis of sex usually justify the practice on the following grounds:

• This discrimination is only temporary.
• The practice is not directed against particular men.
• It is the only way to correct past discrimination against women.

We believe none of these are true justifications. First,

83

what does "temporary" mean? Are we to believe that reverse discrimination against men will be discontinued after a certain date? At whose order? It is difficult to believe that the giant governmental agencies in which this practice is firmly entrenched will give up their vested interests on a given date.

Second, reverse discrimination most certainly *is* directed against particular men, namely, the guys who don't get the job because they're men or who don't receive the same benefits granted to women.

Third, it is very questionable whether a past wrong can or should be corrected by a present injustice. Different people or even generations of people are affected, and the moral of the story is lost. What was a principle becomes a policy — set in stone.

The laws forbidding discrimination are clear and simply stated. They forbid reverse discrimination as well as any other variety of discrimination. Our respect for the law and the courts suffers when a practice that is clearly illegal under the specific words of the law is made to appear legal — even though it eases our conscience.

Making Reverse Discrimination Work for You We do not advocate reverse discrimination of any type. However, many men are discovering their ability to play the reverse discrimination game. Consider the following actual situation:

Laurie is told by a friend and prospective employer that he may have difficulty hiring her. He has hired too many women and fired only men. Complaints have been received that he is practicing sex discrimination.

In such a situation, men may take advantage of an employer's sensitivity to being labeled a "sexist." The chances are good that when a charge of sex discrimination has a basis in fact, the employer will give in.

Some employment classifications continue to be dominated by women. How many bearded secretaries do you encounter? Using the same tactics women have used, men may now be able to insist on preferential treatment.

Illegal Practices

Hiring An employer who refuses to hire men solely because of their sex is violating federal law. This does *not* mean, of course, that federal law guarantees a job to everyone regardless of their qualifications. The point is that any tests used to employ people must measure the person for the job — not the person in the abstract.

Steve applies for a position as a child-care worker in an infant care center. He is refused the job because the director has found that men generally turn their noses up at changing diapers.
Steve's nose is out of joint, he objects, and can expect to win.
The director must evaluate Steve's individual abilities and willingness for the job, not those of men in general.

A large exception to the above rule involves employment situations in which the main purpose of the business would be undermined by not hiring members of one sex exclusively. This exception is called the "bona fide occupational qualification."

Steve tires of babies and decides to work with older children.
He applies for a job as counselor in the local girls' correctional facility. Part of the job involves supervising the teenage girls' showers. Steve will probably be out of luck. Being female is likely to be a "bona fide occupational qualification."

This exception is commonly used to disguise reverse discrimination. Be sure that the "bona fide occupational qualification" relates directly to the actual demands of the job.

Employers charged with discrimination against men will invariably try to justify it as a business necessity. As often as not, of course, it is nothing more than a business convenience or a means of saving money.

The following examples taken from reported law cases illustrate the general rule and the exception to it:

Mr. D. applied to an airline in 1970 for a job as a cabin attendant.
The airline refused the application since they hired only females for such jobs, as indicated by their "Help Wanted — Women" ads. Mr. D. sued the airline, who defended on the ground that women in these jobs were a "business necessity." Mr. D. won his suit; men could do the job as well as women.

In 1972, Mr. S., a registered male nurse, applied to a District of Columbia hospital for private assignments on a first-come-first-served basis. His application was refused because the work included attendance on female patients. Mr. S. sued and won. Such practice by the hospital was discriminatory and illegal.

Pete T., a 50-year-old man experienced in office work, applied for work as a stenographer. He was turned down and later saw an ad for the job under "Help Wanted — Women." When Pete sued, the company maintained that the job was suitable only for women. Pete won.

Again, the Equal Opportunity in Employment laws do not guarantee you employment because you are a man. Equally, an employer is not necessarily guilty of discrimination against you merely because he hired a woman in preference over you.

Dave H. applied for work as an accounting clerk. He was turned down and a woman was hired for the job. Dave sued on the basis of sex discrimination. He lost his lawsuit because the employer was able to show Dave's prior work record was poor, his references were inadequate, and he had not been properly educated for the job.

An employer may refuse to hire an individual whose *status* as a man makes him a poor business risk for the job.

Roger U. applied to a bank for a position in their career-development program that involved at least two years training. His application was refused because of his draft classification, which indicated that he might be inducted into the armed services very shortly. The Equal Opportunities Employment Commission decided that on the facts of this case the bank was justified in refusing Roger's application.

Advertising for Employees Unless an employer needs an employee of a certain sex under the business necessity exception discussed above, his or her ads for employees cannot discriminate against men. This means, for example, that if a job is advertised under "Help Wanted — Women," it must also be advertised under "Help Wanted — Men." Of course, the employer can comply with the law by simply listing the job under "Help Wanted."

Employers cannot ask prospective employees to furnish, in job applications, information regarding their sex, race, marital status, or age. The spirit, if not the letter, of this law is violated frequently by public and private employers. For example, a job description sheet may contain a prominent line stating that "Women and Minorities Are Encouraged to Apply." A box in one of the corners may request applicants to give information as to their sex, handicapped status, and the like. Immediately below, in fine print, the sheet will contain something like, "This information is only *requested*." Sure. Practices such as this should be challenged wherever they appear.

Work Assignments and Classifications Any work assignment or job classification that is based solely on the fact of a man's sex constitutes illegal discrimination.

Men in a Southern California utility company were always assigned to certain physical jobs, and women were assigned to office work. The job descriptions made no mention of any physical or non-physical specifications. A male employee sued, claiming not only that the office work was more desirable but also that it gave employees broader experience to qualify for promotions. The Commission agreed and ordered the practice halted.

Richard T. worked for a Maryland firm that, at the request of its foremen, assigned a certain number of men and a certain number of women to each department. Most of the men wound up in the maintenance and shipping departments, the women in production jobs. This selective classification was held to be discriminatory and illegal.

An employer may not classify a job as "male" or "female" in order to control seniority or promotional opportunities. Nor may an employer classify jobs as "light" or "heavy" to accomplish the same purpose.

However, an employer is not required to treat a man with preference just because the number or percentage of men or women in any given job classification is not in balance.

Ed M. worked for a trucking company in which 90 percent of the office jobs were held by females. Ed claimed these figures alone proved that the company practiced reverse discrimination against men. The Commission disagreed.

87

*Mr. W., an employee of a tire company, requested a transfer
to a job that was earmarked for women and for men with physical
defects. His request was denied. Mr. W. alleged that he would
receive higher pay in the job requested and it would hurt him less
physically. The evidence showed that neither was true and that
the company's refusal to transfer Mr. W. was not discriminatory.*

Women, however, have forced employers to grant
requests such as those described above. Generally, this has
been the result of a voluntary policy of the employer (reverse
discrimination); sometimes quotas have been imposed by
court order for the purpose of correcting past discriminatory
practices.

Fringe Benefits It is illegal for an employer to discriminate
between men and women with regard to fringe benefits.
Such benefits include:
- medical and hospital benefits
- accident, life insurance, and retirement benefits
- profit-sharing and bonus plans
- leave
- any other term or condition of employment

The following examples illustrate this rule:

*The Connecticut State Retirement Act granted women more
favorable considerations in the way retirement benefits were
computed. The act was held to be illegal.*

*Men employed by a New Jersey utility challenged the company's
method of figuring pension plan provisions. Under the plan, a
female could retire on full pension at age 60 with 20 years of service,
but a male was required to be 65 and have worked for 25 years
to receive the same benefits. The company was ordered to raise the
men's benefits to an equal status.*

*Fred L., an employee of an Ohio company, believed his company's
profit-sharing plan discriminated against men. The plan provided
that men could not receive their shares until they were 50 years old
or disabled. Female employees received their benefits when they left
their jobs, regardless of age. The Commission agreed with Fred —
the plan was discriminatory.*

Pregnancy Leave Women are allowed pregnancy leave
under the provisions of almost every employer's medical

plan. The Equal Opportunity in Employment laws have not been interpreted to allow men comparable paternity leave.

Mr. M. worked for the federal government, which gives women pregnancy leave. Mr. M. requested six days paternity leave to participate in the birth of his child at home. The Commission held his request was properly denied since, under federal employment rules, Mr. M. did not have a certifiable medical disability.

Note: This is changing and many employers now grant paternity leave to fathers.

Breaks: Lunch Periods On-the-job benefits such as rest breaks or lunch periods must be equally available to men and women. Former state regulations often afforded women greater benefits in this respect on the assumption that women as a class were inherently weaker than men. Such stereotypes are rejected by federal and state equal employment laws.

Employer Grooming Policies Many employers have a policy, written or unwritten, that requires men to conform to a certain hair length or other grooming standards but makes no such requirement for women. When men have challenged these policies in court or before the Equal Employment Opportunity Commission, the results have been unpredictable. About half of these cases are decided in favor of the men and about half in favor of the employer.

Nevertheless, some generalizations may be made about when such policies will be held to constitute discrimination. First, if the employer can show that certain grooming standards that apply to men only (such as requirements regarding beards, goatees, and sideburns) are related to a safety or health consideration, the policy is probably O.K.

A male welder charged that he was subjected to sex discrimination because he had to shave off his beard. The court held that the rule was a valid occupational qualification based on a reasonable concern for safety. The same result was reached in a case involving a plumbing employee.

Wages Under federal and state civil rights law, the "equal pay for equal work" rule applies. Some state laws still require that overtime pay be provided for female employees and set certain minimum wage standards for women. If your state has such laws, you should challenge them if you're affected. Under present law the state must provide the same wage benefits for male employees in the same positions.

Layoffs It is unlawful for an employer to classify jobs so that a man scheduled for layoff cannot displace a less senior female on a "female" seniority list. For example:

Pete has been with the company 20 years. Jane has been with the company 15 years but is at the top of her female seniority list. Pete, who is near the middle of his "male" seniority list, is scheduled for layoff. He may displace Jane.

If an employer maintains different standards for men and women in connection with discharges, the employer is guilty of discrimination.

An employer and a labor union agreed on a policy regarding layoffs as follows: a male employee, during a layoff situation, could bump another male employee with the least seniority. Female employees, on the other hand, were entitled to bump other employees on the basis of their individual ability to perform the job and were not limited to bumping the least senior employee. This collective bargaining agreement was discriminatory and illegal.

Layoffs are always ugly situations. Women and minorities have only recently secured better jobs than in the past. In seniority-based layoffs they are, unfortunately, the first to go to the unemployment lines. Their new-found economic opportunities are lost and cries of sexism and racism ring loud. While a man may hang on to his job in these situations, he is well advised to stay out of dark alleys.

Promotions and Firings Here again, employers are prohibited from discriminating on the basis of sex. They are required to treat men and women equally. However, they are encouraged to help women succeed and to be very "fair" to women with employment problems. The result is that in this area it is very difficult to prove inequality or reverse discrimination.

Men who are fired are generally incompetent. It is of little value to complain that an equally incompetent female employee would not be fired. (And an employer's difficulty in ridding himself or herself of an inept woman worker is not our subject.)

Many employers astutely give promotional preference to a female over an equally competent male employee. This doesn't hurt the employers and definitely helps their affirmative action statistics. Even when a man is much better qualified for a promotion, proving this is another matter. Employers have never been known for fair or totally objective employment standards. Intangibles such as "working relationships" are also considered, and these will justify almost any practice.

The result is that if you are a man and have missed a promotion because of sex discrimination, you'd better resurrect Clarence Darrow to represent you. If you were fired for reasons other than the fact you are a man, the Equal Opportunity in Employment laws won't help much.

An employer's medical policy placed work restrictions on employees when they were injured or ill. A male employee suffered a medical disability and was terminated. He sued his employer, alleging sex discrimination and pointing out that female employees had been returned to jobs accommodating their disabilities. The EEOC found no discrimination, noting that when the employee returned he had been unable to meet the job classification and had been properly retired for medical reasons.

Social Security Benefits

A number of Social Security benefits that have been denied to men because of their sex have now been granted because the laws were challenged.

For example, there was a provision of the act called the "mother's insurance" provision. It granted benefits to the widow and minor children of a deceased husband, based on his earnings. However, the law provided that if the wife died, benefits were payable only to her minor child and not her husband, based on her earnings. This law was declared to be unconstitutionally discriminatory against men and struck down. Watch for others like it!

On the other hand, the Supreme Court has approved that part of the Social Security law which establishes different and discriminatory criteria for the computation of benefits for men and women at age 62. The Court rationalized this reverse discrimination on the basis that men made more money than women and that higher benefits might induce women to retire earlier. Other judges have described such reasoning as "romantic paternalism."

Property Tax Exemptions

Some states have laws granting widows an annual property tax exemption but offer nothing similar to widowers. These laws have been challenged but, unfortunately for men, have been upheld.

A Florida widower challenged the state's law that granted widows a $500 tax exemption annually but nothing similar to widowers. He took the case to the Supreme Court, which upheld the state law on the basis that a reasonable distinction exists between the financial burden that faces widows and widowers at the time their spouse dies.

You might try to fight such a state law if it is affecting you, but if you win you'll be the first!

Selective Service Classification

At the time of writing, Congress has rejected a bill that would equalize the sexes in regard to compulsory military induction. If the draft does return, we anticipate the "men only" requirement to be hotly contested in the courts.

Fighting Sex Discrimination — and Winning

Cases that involve the more traditional forms of sex discrimination are the easiest to win. You may have the support of fellow male and female employees and of women's groups. For example:

Ron has excellent clerical skills and applies for a secretarial position. He is told, sorry but the company can't hire him. They have only one washroom, and that's for ladies only.

In reverse discrimination cases you will allege that female employees are getting a better deal than you. This is likely to cause your female friends to desert you. The agencies set up to help you or to hear your case will probably be less than sympathetic to your position.

Take a lesson from women. Don't just complain — act. The anti-discrimination and complaints procedures are set up for *your* benefit also. Enlist the support of other men who may be in similar positions. Employers and bureaucrats, when confronted with a well-organized and prepared group, will be more likely to follow the law.

Negotiate with Your Employer If you are a man and the victim of reverse discrimination in employment, the fastest and least expensive way to go, obviously, is to try and correct the discriminatory practice by negotiating with your employer. Almost every employer these days is very aware of the problems posed by discriminatory practices against minorities and is well informed on how to deal with them. Employers generally may be less informed about reverse discrimination and how to handle it.

When you confront your employer or your employer's representative with your complaint, you'd better have your facts straight. If, for example, you are seeking to equalize discriminatory pension plan provisions, you should have at your fingertips the details of the plan and the benefits paid out under it. And if you claim the right to displace a female employee by reason of your seniority in a layoff situation, you'll need the seniority lists with dates, names, and so on. If you need documents you don't have or can't get easily, demand the information from your employer. He or she may refuse, in which case you'll be able to obtain the information in a formal proceeding.

Your employer may flatly deny your charges. If so — and your complaint is valid — the next step is to take formal action. Your employer may investigate your allegation and take corrective action. If so, all well and good. But the chances are better that your employer will concede some of your points but be fearful of taking action out of a fear of angering the women and minority employees. That's not your problem. Your problem is to convince your employer that the practice has to be corrected, or you'll see each other in court. It's going to cost time and money and, if your contentions are valid, your employer will lose anyway. Make this very clear.

Next Step: The EEOC Don't phone your lawyer yet; you may spend money unnecessarily. If your employer has given you no satisfaction, you should immediately contact by phone or letter the closest district office near you of the Equal Employment Opportunity Commission (called the EEOC). The address of this office should be posted on your job. If it's not, ask your personnel office. In any event, it is listed under "U.S. Government" in the white pages of the telephone directory.

The EEOC is a federal administrative agency that is charged with the duty of combating discrimination in employment. Many states also have parallel state agencies that will get involved in discrimination cases. Ask the federal office you call or write whether the state in which you live has such an agency you must contact.

A note of caution here. Many EEOC personnel view sex discrimination as something only experienced by women. They may have a heart attack when a man asks for help. If so, wait until they recover, offer your sympathies, and press on.

The EEOC district office will send you a form entitled "Charge of Discrimination." Simply fill it out in clear, simple language using your own words. Do not muddle it up with legalese. The EEOC will even accept a written statement from you instead of the form, provided the statement gives sufficient information to identify the parties, describes the alleged discriminatory practices, and so on. It is not necessary that you personally file this form or statement. It may be filed on your behalf by another person, organization, or group.

The federal EEOC must refer your complaint to your state's fair employment practices agency if there is one. That agency has 60 days to act on your complaint.

If there is no such state agency or if there is one and no action is taken on your complaint, the EEOC takes over the process. The EEOC notifies your employer that you have filed charges and investigates your complaint.

If the EEOC agrees with you that you are the victim of discrimination, the agency will try and negotiate a settlement with your employer. If this is unsuccessful, the EEOC may file a court action against your employer or you may file one privately.

Note: Your right to file such charges is protected by law. Your employer may not seek revenge for your filing by taking any unjustified action against you. If this happens, contact the EEOC or your attorney and report it.

When to File a Court Action After your charges are filed, if the EEOC has not completed its investigation and attempts to settle the matter, the agency will send you a form notifying you of your "right to sue." If you are going ahead with a court action, you must start it within *90 days* after receipt of this notice.

Note: Under recent court decisions you will not have to prove that your employer acted in "bad faith"; that is, that there was intentional discrimination against you. This makes your court case much easier to win.

Attorneys Numerous lawyers specialize in labor matters and are extremely proficient in handling labor discrimination cases. Less numerous, perhaps, are those who handle reverse discrimination cases. In cases involving traditional sex discrimination, rather than reverse discrimination, women's rights organizations and attorneys specializing in women's issues may be particularly helpful.

If you have been fired from your job because of reverse discrimination, your lawyer will of course seek damages. If you are still working, the case should be less complicated and cost you less, since your lawyer will probably not be seeking money but a court order halting the practice.

As in divorce proceedings, it may be strategic to obtain the services of a good female laywer to represent you. She may be able to act as a buffer to the inevitable charge that you are only a damned man trying to set back women's rights a hundred years.

Points to Remember in Fighting Sex Discrimination

- Make your employer or prospective employer aware of the problem.
- Let the employer know you are serious.
- Enlist the support of other men and employees.
- Don't be afraid to use the Equal Employment Opportunity Commission (EEOC) and the courts. They exist for you also.
- Don't fall into the "sexist" trap of feeling that you must give women a break.
- Don't apologize for insisting on equal rights.

Remember: employers, regulatory agencies, and lawmakers generally will only give you what you demand.

PART II

DIVORCE AND SEPARATION: THE PARTNERS

7
Going to Court

Only two out of ten divorce cases are contested and decided by a judge. But if your case is one of those two, these odds aren't relevant. Rational people dread going to court — for any reason, and if the battle is a family matter, the skeletons really come rattling out of the closet. Unless you're an exceptionally secure man, you'd be well advised to have some support systems going for you as well as a good lawyer. We recommend that you have someone (a good friend, say) to lean on during the court trial of a divorce — someone with whom you can really let off steam or even tell that you're miserable.

It may not be as bad as you think, or it may be worse. Everything depends, of course, on the circumstances of your case, the attorneys, the judge, and the law in your state. You've tried to work out an agreement before going to court, and that hasn't been successful. But at least the negotiations have given you and your attorney a pretty good idea of what your wife's case will look like. Better the devil you know. . . .

Men's Organizations

One source of help and support may be the various men's organizations that have recently come into existence. Some of these organizations are somewhat frivolous; others are dedicated and serious. Unlike most of the women's organizations, the men's organizations that do exist are still only fledgling attempts to provide men — especially men undergoing divorce proceedings — with advice and help. Many are understaffed (if staffed at all) and are maintained by volunteer attorneys and various reform-minded individuals. And they generally lack the political power and common purpose found in so many women's organizations. (A good article on this subject may be found in *Playboy*, December 1978, p. 213: "Who Gets Screwed in a Divorce? I Do!" by Asa Babar.)

In the Appendix, at the back of the book, you will find a list of men's organizations that we believe will be helpful. They should be able to provide you with information concerning the laws of your state and appropriate referrals, should you need them.

Grounds for Divorce

Only three states still require that divorce be based on fault: Illinois, Pennsylvania, and South Dakota.

More than thirty-five states now have specific no-fault divorce laws. *No fault* means that parties seeking to divorce need only allege (state in the complaint or petition) that the marriage has "irretrievably" broken down, that they have "irreconcilable differences," or something similar.

In the states that have retained fault as a ground for divorce, the spouse who is not "at fault" often receives more than his or her normal share of the marital property and, in some cases, custody of the children.

Fault, in these states, can mean a lot of things, including criminal acts, fraud, and abandonment. Usually, though, it refers to adultery. In a fault state, if both spouses want a divorce, they would traditionally set up a fake adultery situation involving, almost always, the man. He would be "discovered" in the adulterous act or situation, and his wife would file for divorce. This crazy charade has largely been discarded in those states where it was once the norm, but it still goes on to some extent. If you find yourself in such a situation and agree, for your own reasons, to go through with such an act, you'd better make a binding settlement with your wife before the court action.

Defenses to Divorce

The trend has been to eliminate defenses to divorce, particularly the traditional defenses. And since the advent of no-fault divorce, this trend has accelerated. Of course, you may not be interested in defending against the divorce if your wife has filed. On the other hand, you may.

Practically every state has minimized the number of defenses available to a spouse fighting a divorce. Some of the states that have eliminated defenses entirely are:

Arizona	District of	Montana
California	Columbia	Oregon
Colorado	Indiana	Virgin Islands
Delaware	Kentucky	Wisconsin
	Missouri	

Certain states, such as Minnesota, Ohio, and Utah, have no laws on the books authorizing defenses, but court decisions have established certain defenses. Your attorney will need to advise you as to the status of the law in your state.

Reconciliation?

One of the first subjects a good attorney will discuss with you is the possibility of reconciliation. This may anger you or make you want to change attorneys. But a word of caution: You should doubt an attorney who does *not* discuss reconciliation with you.

Men, like women, can get stubborn and angry when hurt. All right, but don't let that get in your way when considering reconciliation. You have nothing to prove to your lawyer; your pride and anger are immaterial. If you feel — even slightly — that there is a *chance* you might patch it up with your wife, tell your lawyer and take a while to think it over. It's your *life and happiness* that's at stake, not your lawyer's.

There's nothing as expensive and damaging than trying to reconcile with your wife halfway through a divorce suit. When your case starts, you will essentially be taking an adversary position to one another, and insults will be heaped on indignities. The possibilities of reconciliation will fade under the pressure of the lawsuit you both want to win. Decide whether you may want to reconcile *now* — before it's too late. If you need counseling, try to persuade your wife to participate. After all, what do either of you really have to lose — except a miserable lawsuit?

Several states, including Illinois, Indiana, Kansas, Ohio, and Texas, have laws that provide for a delay or a cooling-off period before a divorce trial may begin. The delays vary from three to six months. The purpose of these laws, of course, is to give the parties time to think it over and, perhaps, to reconcile before they go any further.

Some of these states also have mandatory conciliation proceedings, in which a court commissioner requires both parties to attend at least one private, informal conference to explore the possibilities of reconciliation. Usually this procedure is initiated by at least one of the parties indicating his or her desire for such a meeting. If you're interested in knowing more about such procedures in your state, ask your attorney.

Legal Separation

Legal separation (often called "separate maintenance") may suit the needs of men whose religious persuasion does not allow divorce. And, in some instances, a legal separation may be suitable when husband and wife are not totally committed to ending their relationship permanently.

Legal separation has fallen into disuse in recent years, particularly since no-fault divorce has become common. One reason for this is that the legal separation requires a separate maintenance action in which the same issues must be decided as in a divorce case (custody, spousal and child support, and property division). Most people are unwilling to go through all this without ending their relationship.

In a legal separation, the spouses — by agreement or court order — separate and live apart. A couple will experience little additional delay or expense should they decide to divorce rather than separate. Most states provide that at the end of a specified time, usually the same as that required for a divorce to become final, either spouse may request that the legal separation action be converted to a divorce action and that the court issue a final decree or judgment of divorce.

If you are interested in this alternative to divorce, ask your lawyer about the details.

Do You Need an Attorney?

The answer is yes, except possibly in the case of an uncontested divorce, and even then you may need an attorney to draw up a marital settlement agreement or advise you how to do it yourself. The cost of legal representation in divorce actions is outrageous. However, to suggest that the average man walk into the courtroom to present his own case would be like sending a lamb into a lion's den.

The chances are good that if you represent yourself you may lose your case before you even get into court. Most trial work is won or lost in pretrial preparation and maneuvers (discovery procedures, motions, requests for temporary orders, restraining orders, and so on) which simply cannot be summed up for the average man. As expensive and wasteful as it might be, if your wife has an attorney and there's *anything* important at stake, you'd better cave in and hire a lawyer yourself.

If You Try Your Own Case   Still, some men — for various reasons — want to try their own cases. If you're one of these, the best advice we can give you is to find a friendly legal secretary who does family law work and is willing to give you advice (and possibly loan you books). Also, check for paralegal help. Many paralegal people are very familiar with the nonsensical intricacies of legal procedure and can simplify them for you.

You may receive some assistance from sympathetic court personnel (the judge's clerk, the filing clerk, and so on), but you may equally well get a cold shoulder. Many court employees consider it an affront to their entire system of values to deal with a lay person.

Last but not least, try to find some men's organizations in

your state that may help (such as Equal Rights for Fathers).

Assuming you get to court on your own, you'll have to familiarize yourself with the rules of evidence and trial procedure that apply in your state. And in all probability you'll have to overcome the hostility of the judge. Judges usually hate to deal with amateur lawyers; they complicate the trial immeasurably.

In any event, good luck!

Uncontested Divorces: Defaults Although we recommend that you be legally represented in court proceedings, uncontested divorces are the exception.

Uncontested means one of two things. First, it may mean that the person against whom the divorce action has been filed has not responded at all to the papers or summons. In that case, the person filing the divorce will be granted a "default" judgment or decree of divorce that generally awards what that person has asked for in the complaint or petition.

Uncontested is also used to describe a situation in which the parties have made an agreement, and all that remains is for a judge to approve the agreement and issue the judgment or decree in open court with only one person present. This is sometimes called a "judgment by stipulation." The work is all done in the lawyers' offices, negotiating the best agreement possible. As this is written, California has enacted a law effective January 1, 1981, under which neither the parties nor their attorneys need appear in court at all.

In any event, you should not need an attorney to handle an uncontested divorce once an agreement is reached. In most states, the procedure simply is that your case is placed on a calendar of uncontested matters and called on a certain date. (Some states call these "law and motion calendars.") When your case is called, the judge reads the substance of the petition, verifies the fact that an agreement was made and approves it, goes through a little more legal hocus-pocus, and issues the judgment or decree. This procedure varies from state to state in minor respects.

It is usually up to you to file the judgment and send a copy of it to your wife. Later, of course, you must apply for the final decree and go through the same procedure.

If you are taking an uncontested divorce against your wife and have no attorney, check with any paralegal people you can find. Or ask a legal secretary, if you know one. It is also possible that the court may issue pamphlets on the procedure, since it is so widespread. It is not a particularly complicated procedure, but it must be done correctly.

Finding and Working with an Attorney

How to Find the Right One   For many men who are getting divorced, finding an attorney who is diligent, honest, and doesn't cost an arm and a leg is as difficult as dealing with the whole idea of divorce itself. Unfortunately, divorce proceedings usually attract a more predatory, more unethical sort of lawyer than any other kind of litigation. This may be because men have traditionally been required to pay attorney's fees for both themselves and their wives. And divorcing couples are easy marks; they are often defensive, guilty, unhappy, and lonely.

Another part of the deserved reputation of divorce lawyers is connected with the traditional nature of the proceedings. A woman in tears calls on Mr. Shark and pours out her story of heartbreak and outrage. Mr. Shark, an old veteran, comforts her, dries her tears, assures her justice will be done, and tells her everything else she wants to hear — assuming, that is, that she or her husband has a fat bank account.

In any event, there's little you can do about your wife's lawyer, but there *is* a lot you can do about your own. The best plan is to get a good recommendation from another man who has been through the mill. The next best is probably to obtain a recommendation from an attorney you know or one who has handled other matters for you.

Many urban areas have group legal practices. These are legal assistance groups sponsored by consumer action groups, employers, unions, and the like that offer legal assistance at discount rates. But be very careful about relying on these groups — many are mediocre, at best.

Most cities have lawyer referral services, some sponsored by state bar associations and others not. Our advice generally is to avoid such referral services. Lawyers are listed simply because they choose to be; there is absolutely no guarantee that you will obtain adequate representation. If you use such services, you're no better off than looking through the telephone book (or the ads, in states where lawyers can advertise) or picking a name out of a hat.

If none of the above suggestions works for you, try one of the men's organizations listed at the end of the book. Many provide legal referral services and try to evaluate the lawyers who are members. You might even try NOW (National Organization of Women). Yes, they *will* help you if they can.

You should give serious consideration to having a woman attorney represent you, particularly if your divorce may involve facts that traditionally produce sympathy for the woman. A woman attorney may be able to act as a buffer between you and your wife and her attorney. Again, a women's organization may be helpful here.

It is common for men to use their wife's attorney, hoping to save another fee. *Don't do this.* Her lawyer has agreed to represent *her* in what are essentially adversary proceedings. If you could be represented by the same lawyer, he or she would be violating the Code of Ethics. This is a horrible way to try to save a buck — it may wind up costing you a bundle.

Fees Attorney's fees vary so much from state to state, and even from city to city, that any generalization on fair fees may be useless to you in your specific situation. Hourly fees range from $50–200 an hour; court appearances cost from $200–1,000 or more. Most attorneys will not take divorce work on a contingency basis (that is, they get paid only if their clients win and are awarded fees); most will bill you for their hours spent plus a fee for each court appearance.

In all likelihood, your attorney will require a retainer (payment in advance), which may run from $100 to $5,000, depending on the complexities of your case. Few divorce attorneys will start work with only your promise to pay.

You'll probably see some advertisements in which

divorces are "handled" for $150 or some equally ridiculous sum. Avoid these so-called bargain rates. Sad but true, you get what you pay for.

Other Legal Costs   In addition to attorney's fees, there may be costs for obtaining the services of expert witnesses (such as physicians or accountants), as well as minor expenses (mileage and the like) involved in calling ordinary witnesses. And, of course, there are court costs, such as filing fees, subpoena fees, and transcript fees.

In most instances, attorneys require that clients advance these costs to them.

Your First Conference   Your attorney must examine several legal aspects of your divorce case immediately. These include: how long you have lived where you do, vital statistics for you and your wife, the ground for divorce (if necessary), custody and support of the children, alimony, property division, and the need for any temporary protective orders. Your lawyer will question you closely on these matters and others, to determine as well as possible whether conciliation may be advised.

At this initial conference, you will be advised as to fees, the lawyer's method of billing, and (hopefully) the maximum fee involved. Fees are discussed in more detail later. Your attorney should also give you a general overview of the rules in your state that govern custody, support, and property division.

If you have initiated the divorce and wish to spare your wife undue embarrassment, you should ask your attorney to have her served in your attorney's office if that seems feasible. If she already has an attorney, her attorney may accept process on her behalf (in some states this is not permissible for the first summons).

Many good attorneys, particularly experienced ones, prefer to paint a somewhat pessimistic picture at the initial conference of their clients' chances of obtaining what they want. This is to counteract the rosy picture most people have of their own cases. Most of us clearly see our own contentions

107

in any conflict and rationalize them as the only reasonable arguments possible. Good lawyers will sharply point out to their clients the possibilities on the other side. In order to represent and negotiate effectively, lawyers must know the weaknesses, as well as the strengths, of their clients' cases. Better to discover these in the office than in the courtroom!

Even if you live in a fault state, your lawyer should not base the entire case on the theory that your wife's fault caused the divorce and that she is therefore blameworthy in every respect. For example, if your wife has engaged in adultery and your lawyer tries to use that fact alone to prove she is an unfit mother, you will probably lose on the custody issue.

Don't goad your lawyer into this kind of unproductive stance by advocating "going after the bitch." It may make you feel better to see this happen, but your good feeling will disappear rapidly when you lose your case (and see your attorney's bill). The best thing your lawyer can do in court is to identify with and understand the position of the judge — not of you or your wife. And the judge probably doesn't want to hear a long recital of the other person's faults from either of you.

Level with your lawyer. You have absolutely *nothing* to gain by hiding or evasion. Your lawyer is your employee; it makes no more sense to delude your lawyer than to delude yourself. There is nothing more devastating to a lawsuit than what lawyers call "surprise" — having a pivotal fact sprung on them in the courtroom for which they are totally unprepared. *Never* play such games with your own lawyer.

Evaluating Your Lawyer's Work What are some of the ways to tell if the lawyer you've hired is doing a good job? There are many, but probably none are as good as your gut feelings. Here are some questions you can ask yourself; if the answer to more than one or two is "no," you'd better think of changing lawyers. Has your lawyer:
- obtained all the documents and papers you feel are essential for a thorough understanding of your divorce?
- talked to all the persons you feel could help your case (school personnel, friends, work associates, doctors, counselors, and so on)?

- obtained an adequate background understanding of your marriage and how it came to fail?
- talked with the children, if possible and appropriate, and gained a realistic picture of how they feel and what they prefer?
- kept you informed as to the legal stages your case is in and why?
- leveled with you as to costs and fees?
- found out necessary information about the judge who will try your case?
- adequately explained to you the legal procedures and laws of your state?

Changing Lawyers Never be afraid to change lawyers when you feel it is imperative. You may be wrong in your assessment of your attorney's capabilities or you may be right. Your lawyer may be able to charm the birds off the trees, and perhaps you are the one who can't get along. But no matter; you cannot work with an attorney you're not comfortable with, you have little or no confidence in, or you just don't get along with.

You have a *right* to change lawyers — even in midstream. It will cost you, however. Before your lawyer signs off the case, you'll probably be required to pay any fees that are due. And part of those fees will be for the legal work involved in bringing in another lawyer. Still, it's worth it. There's a lot at stake, and you shouldn't pennypinch at this stage of the game.

A word of caution is in order: Some of the best attorneys are relatively uncommunicative and will not tell you stories designed to make you feel better. And this is not your lawyer's job; lawyers are not counselors. Don't let this throw you off. Your lawyer's ability will be tested in court, not by reassuring you beforehand.

Before Trial

The most important thing to remember about the pretrial period in a divorce case is not to discuss the case or your feelings about it with anyone other than your attorney. This goes for your business and personal friends, relatives, school personnel, physicians, and casual acquaintances. You don't have to become paranoid, but you must be careful about telephone conversations with strangers or people you don't trust.

Many men facing a divorce trial tell no one (except their attorneys) where they can be reached. You may or may not feel this is necessary, but in any event it's a good idea to rent a private post-office box to receive your correspondence.

By this time, you should have already cancelled all joint credit cards and closed all joint bank accounts. Your creditors will probably be aware of the impending lawsuit and may be getting nervous. Any debts for which you are liable — either individually or jointly — must be paid, of course. But you can't afford to have creditors bothering you before the trial. Your attorney and your wife's attorney should work out an interim method of satisfying joint debts pending conclusion of the trial.

You should simply let your children know you will be going to court (they'll know anyway), but don't discuss the details with them. Let them know that they are not responsible for your divorce and that they can love both you and their mother. But be prepared for some acting-out behavior by them.

If you have been ordered out of the house by the court, keep visiting your children (unless you have been restrained by court order from visitation) until the trial ends. But *never* take your children from the home unless you have temporary visitation rights that permit you to do so. And if you have temporary custody of your children, allow their mother reasonable visitation unless the court orders differently.

Case Investigation If agreement seems impossible and your divorce case will be determined by a trial on the merits (the evidence submitted to the judge), your attorney should make a detailed investigation. This includes, often, taking your wife's deposition (oral questions answered under oath and recorded) and interviews with and statements by witnesses that relate to marital misconduct or fitness for custody (if relevant). School records should be obtained when necessary in custody cases. Bank records and ownership of property should be examined. A private investigator may be required to establish your claim of adultery or other misconduct (in those states where such grounds are required). Often, interviews with physicians or psychiatrists may be necessary.

Witnesses Most judges will pay little attention to your testimony if it is directly contradicted by your wife's testimony. This is particularly true if you must produce proof of your wife's misconduct to justify the divorce. Consequently, it is important that you obtain witnesses to corroborate your testimony on matters relating to misconduct, indignities, cruelty, and fitness for custody.

Your lawyer may plan (without knowing it) to call witnesses who are intensely partisan to you. If any of your witnesses fall into this category, make sure your lawyer knows who they are so that they can be warned in advance not to exaggerate or give the impression they are sacrificing the truth for the sake of friendship (or for the sake of hostility toward your wife).

Other Relationships You may or may not have a relationship with another woman at the time of your trial. If you live in a state where no fault is required for divorce, we see no reason to hide the relationship or deny its existence. For one thing, you may not care to lie. Furthermore, your wife's attorney will, in all probability, discover it anyway and you'll look foolish.

The issue of child custody, even though you live in a no fault state, may require that your personal life be examined — insofar as it is relevant to the question of the best interests of the child. In short, even though your relationship with another woman may not be attacked in court directly, some facts about your lifestyle and domicile arrangements may be discussed as they relate to other issues.

Regardless of the state in which your case is being tried,

it makes good sense not to flaunt any extramarital relationship. Your private life is of course your own and may not disqualify you as a custodial parent, but it is well to remember that sexual promiscuity has been viewed by many judges as an important factor in determining custody.

Keeping Mind and Body Together During the Trial

Once your case comes to trial, every day attorneys will be digging into the ruins of your marriage somewhat like archeologists and discovering and reconstructing bits of facts. From the facts, they will present their interpretations of your intentions, character, relationships, finances, and prospects. The history of your marriage will probably be traced — from your beginning hopes to the alienation and disillusionment that came in the end. And throughout the dreary courtroom dissection of your marital failures, you must maintain control.

Out of Court The physical and emotional strain will be immense. It is a good idea to leave the courtroom behind you each day and go to work out at your favorite gym or health club, or participate in some other form of exercise that appeals to you. You'll find the exercise invigorating, and it will free your mind somewhat from the terrors that await you the next day. Get as much rest as you can under the circumstances. The amount of nervous energy you expend in court — just sitting and listening — would surprise you.

Probably the most difficult thing men have to fight in divorce cases is their own loneliness. While in court, you'll find that the adrenalin keeps you on edge; afterwards, depression and a feeling of isolation may begin to haunt you. You'll probably feel that no one, including your attorney, *really* understands what this is costing you emotionally; you will probably also feel that the court hearing will never end. Remember: other men have been through the same thing or worse, and it *does* end.

We do not recommend intensive counseling sessions during your court trial. At this time it is more important for you to get through the stress of the proceedings than to probe your motivations and feelings. A contested divorce trial is a miserable, petty, and painful experience. No amount of alcohol, Valium, or "getting in touch with your feelings" will lessen this reality. Perhaps the most helpful thing to you at this time will be the company of a good friend.

In Court   Your task in court is to make an effective *personal* presentation to the judge, and your attorney's task is to make an effective *legal* presentation to the judge.

Your case will be decided by the facts presented, not by histrionics or Perry Mason tactics. The judge will probably have heard every complaint a bitter husband can make and witnessed every legal maneuver in a lawyer's bag of tricks. Neither will work. The judge will also be very used to the conflicting testimony of divorcing spouses and is likely to take what either of you say with a grain of salt.

Present yourself as a respectful and attentive person, but do not be overawed or too deferential. Do not glare, smirk, mutter, or otherwise draw attention to yourself while your wife (or anyone else for that matter) is testifying. Just listen carefully to what the witness is saying. Obviously you must *never* interrupt a witness, regardless of how outrageous the testimony may be. Remember, if you can, that the woman on the stand testifying is the woman you married once — long ago.

No matter what the circumstances are, you owe her and each witness in the courtroom civility and decency. If there's to be any bad-mouthing, leave it to others. Nobody is going to come out of the courtroom a real winner, so conduct yourself with some class.

Be responsive to questions when you are a witness. Don't volunteer additional information or your opinion. These will be asked for when needed. It is your attorney's job to ask you relevant questions, and there are likely to be good reasons for *not* asking you certain questions.

Follow the same strategy when you are questioned by your

wife's attorney, who will probably try to get you rattled, to be defensive, and to contradict yourself. Even if these tactics are successful, remember it is the judge who makes the decision. The judge will have seen the same thing happen to countless other witnesses and will have long ago stopped expecting witnesses to be perfect.

Your attorney will present the facts of your case and attempt to have the legal rules interpreted in your favor. However, most of this work should have been done before the trial. If you have leveled with your attorney and if the pretrial investigation was adequate, the trial should hold few surprises.

You can help your attorney most by relinquishing any claim to be the expert in courtroom strategy. Do not whisper constantly in your attorney's ear, cleverly pointing out inconsistencies in your wife's testimony, and reminding your attorney to ask her certain questions.

Listen carefully to all the testimony given and, when the witness concludes, converse with your attorney as necessary at the counsel table. If you have something urgent to say, see if your attorney can obtain a short recess.

In the rare instances where your children may be asked questions in open court (usually this is done in the judge's chambers), be supportive of them, no matter how much it hurts. There is no way the kids are even remotely responsible for what is happening; be sure they realize it.

Your Wife's Attorney: Control Yourself   Of all the people you meet during the divorce process, you will hate none more than your wife's attorney. Some of the reasons for this are logical, and others are not.

Your wife's attorney represents *her* in an adversary proceeding (and that's what contested divorce is, regardless of what you may read). This person's job is to win for your wife — which means that you lose. No matter how cool and collected you may be, this won't enthrall you. The methods your wife's attorney may use to win are of infinite variety, but *win is the name of the game.* (By *win*, we mean obtain the court order or judgment favorable to the client.) Her attorney, in all probability, is experienced and has done this before so many times it has become automatic. You will be presented as the bad guy. This will be the theme, and bad guys just don't deserve much.

Insinuating questions, sneering derogation of your answers, the arched eyebrow, the "involuntary" smirk — these and other tactics may drive you up the wall. Don't let them! The judge won't be impressed by the histrionics of either attorney, nor their judgment calls. Your lawyer will protect you insofar as the rules of evidence and courtroom procedure permit, but a great deal will be up to you. Remember that both attorneys will probably have a drink together after the trial.

After the Trial

Nobody really wins a divorce trial. In fact, everybody loses. Be that as it may, you may have obtained custody and support orders favorable to you, unfavorable to you, or, most likely, just mediocre. You probably will walk out of the courtroom feeling you were treated unfairly; so will your wife.

Contrary to some popular stereotypes, studies have shown that as a general rule divorce is harder emotionally on men than on women. More men than women go off the deep end after divorce; more drink excessively or commit suicide. Perhaps part of the reason for this is that many men have so few close relationships. Once a man becomes vulnerable in a relationship and this relationship is shattered, he may literally have no place to go. This is exacerbated by his training, which, of course, has been to mask his emotions and suppress his feelings. Many men, unable to cope effectively with the loss of their families, also lose interest in their jobs and future. As a general rule, on the other hand, women — though initially often crushed by the end of a marriage — seem to have more ability to shake it off and go ahead as best they can.

If you have lost custody of your children, remember that no piece of paper issued by a court can affect your feelings about your children or theirs about you. As hard as it may be, remember also that in some respects this is chapter one of your *new* life, as well as the last chapter of your old life. Of *course* you will be depressed, but at least the air is cleared. The children won't disappear, nor will they be hostile toward you — often quite the opposite. Also, custody orders are never final. A lot can happen on the way to being a single parent — and that goes for your wife as well.

8
Marital Settlement Agreements

Four out of every five divorces in the United States are uncontested; that is, they are settled out of court. Most of these involve the same bitterness and sadness as contested cases, and all involve the same crucial issues of spousal support, child custody, support and visitation, and property division.

In an uncontested divorce, the issues are negotiated by the couple and their attorneys before going to court. The written agreement that they make is called a "marital settlement agreement." (Other terms commonly used are *divorce settlements, property settlements,* and *separation agreements.*) This agreement is submitted to the judge and, if approved, is incorporated into the final judgment or decree ending the marriage.

Even though a divorce may be uncontested and the issues resolved by mutual agreement, there are still problems, differences, and hard feelings to be dealt with. Few couples can separate without losses to both parties. Each generally feels that he or she has lost more than is fair. And generally this is the case.

A marital settlement agreement (referred to in this chapter as an "agreement") is usually the least expensive, quickest, easiest, most flexible, and most amicable means of resolving the issues of a failed marriage.

Another advantage of such an agreement is that it allows you and your wife to dispose of matters over which the judge has little control, such as insurance and estate planning.

What to Do If You Can't Agree

Generally, plain common sense and healthy self-interest motivate couples to make marital settlement agreements. Hopefully, husband and wife decide — or at least accept — that their marriage is finished and they want to begin a new chapter of their lives as cheaply and painlessly as possible.

But when couples can't agree, husband and wife present their cases separately and in the end the court decides. This is a bitter, time-consuming process:

Rick and Linda's attempt to work out their divorce rationally broke down when they tried to divide the "his and her" towels. Both ran to their attorneys. A property inventory was made, at a cost of $1,500. Investigators were hired, at a cost of $800. A child custody investigation was ordered by the court, at a cost of $150. Other costs: $1,100. Total attorneys' fees: $10,300. Total cost of the divorce: $13,850. Time involved: 18 months. Result: Rick, Linda, and their child are poorer and still unhappy with the way things worked out.

Rick and Linda could have made sensible concessions and saved themselves a lot of money. The distribution of their property and support obligations could have been tailored to the needs of each person and each tax situation, rather than simply imposed by a judge. Equally important, they would not have wasted eighteen months of their lives fighting over a relationship that had already ended.

Obviously, sometimes a marital settlement *is* impossible. Your wife may refuse to negotiate or she may make excessive demands. Or you may have a genuine disagreement about a matter as important as child custody. Remember that even then you can agree on some issues and leave the court to decide the rest. For example, Rick and Linda could have agreed on child custody and fought only the property and support issues in court.

Kinds of Agreements

Not all marital settlement agreements are the same. To some degree your agreement will depend on where you live, but, more important, the type of agreement you make will reflect the individual wishes of you and your wife.

Integrated Agreements   In an integrated agreement, both persons agree on provisions for support in exchange for mutual promises on division of property. The provisions are made in consideration of one another. The result is that the support provisions are then part and parcel of the division of property, and it is *immaterial whether the property is divided equally*. In short, the result has been reached by mutual bargaining.

For example:

Bernie owns half the family house and would be obligated to pay spousal support. He promises to give his wife his interest in the house in exchange for her promise to give up spousal support.

Integrated agreements usually contain the following:
- a clause that both persons intend to reach a final settlement of all rights and duties
- a waiver clause (waiver means "give up") under which one party agrees to give up his or her rights except as spelled out in the agreement
- a statement that each provision of the agreement is made in consideration of the other provision (the result of bargaining)

Note: Whatever the terms of the agreement, it is *not* final with regard to child support. The court always has the power to change an agreement in that respect. In fact, in a few states the court can also change the spousal support provision under certain circumstances.

Severable Agreements   In a severable agreement (sometimes called "separable"), the provisions for support are completely independent of the provisions for the division of property. In other words, each provision stands on its own without reference to the other provisions, which is not the case in integrated agreements. For example:

Jack and Sarah own a house worth $50,000 and other property worth $50,000. Jack agrees to take the house, and Sarah agrees to take the other property. Jack also agrees to pay Sarah $200 a month as spousal support.

This agreement is severable — each person took an equal

share in property and Jack's spousal support has no relationship to the property division. *These agreements should be avoided,* chiefly because they always leave open the issue of spousal support for future change.

Limited Agreements

Mark and Gretchen together own and manage a restaurant. And both want to continue in the restaurant — without the other. While the court will have to decide about the restaurant, Mark and Gretchen do agree that Mark should have custody of their 13-year-old son. They make a limited agreement to that effect.

As mentioned earlier, you need not agree on everything involved in the divorce to make a marital settlement agreement. For example, you and your wife may be able to agree on child custody, support, and visitation, but unable to agree on spousal support. Or you may agree on all of these but not on the division of property. The matters on which you cannot reach agreement will be tried by the court at a hearing.

Do You *Need* an Agreement?

Mike and Carolyn have been married one year and plan an uncontested divorce. They both work, and they have saved $1,000, which they plan to split equally. They have no other property and no children. Neither claims spousal support.

Obviously, if this couple needs a marital settlement agreement, it need not be complicated or expensive. In many states, the agreement will consist of filling in the blank spaces on one of the papers served together with the summons. In other states, the clerk of the court will ask the parties to fill out a "short-form" property settlement agreement. Both of these methods are designed for couples like Mike and Carolyn, and such summary agreements are perfectly satisfactory.

The need for a formal marital settlement agreement increases with the complexities of the particular financial situation. Substantial assets, children, debts, a disparity between the incomes of the spouses, non-monetary contributions to the marriage — these are some of the matters that require a formal agreement.

If you're tempted to forget the whole thing and make a verbal agreement, remember that just because you're divorced doesn't necessarily mean you'll never have to deal with your partner again. Various claims can be made against you later by your former wife that do not depend on the situation at the time you were divorced. And in some instances, claims against you can be made by her heirs or dependents. If you're in doubt at all, make a written agreement, even if it's a do-it-yourself contract.

Is an Attorney Necessary?

A marital property settlement is a contract that will affect you, your children, and even your future wife, if you remarry, for a long time. An attorney is *necessary*, in our opinion, for a settlement in which any of the following matters are at issue:
  • child custody, support, or visitation
  • spousal support
  • ownership and disposition of property (including debts) valued at more than $2,000

If you have few assets, have been married a relatively short time, have no children, and spousal support will not be relevant, make your own agreement. *But,* you must familiarize yourself with the requirements in your state that apply to such agreements. We suggest you first ask the clerk of the court (domestic relations) and then seek any available paralegal help. In many states, there is a legal secretary's handbook that contains the proper forms, as well as instructions on how to fill them out and file them.

Attorneys working out a property settlement agreement will ask for a retainer and bill you by the hour. If any court appearances are required, they will be extra. Our advice: when in doubt, hire a lawyer!

Who Pays Attorney's Fees? In a divorce case, the husband traditionally pays all the attorney's fees. Although the law in most states now permits judges to award attorney's fees as they see fit, the man still pays more often than not. This may be used as leverage against you in settlement negotiations, particularly if your wife has obtained a preliminary order commanding you to pay at least part of these fees.

Resist this leverage and, if necessary, threaten to take the issue to court rather than give in. Demand that you each pay your own attorney's fees. The law is changing on this point; be aggressive.

This particular battle is worth winning for at least two reasons. First, if you lose, you'll be in for a bath, in all probability. You'd be surprised at what a clever lawyer can do to "prove" $10,000 worth of legal work was necessary!

Second, and perhaps equally important — watch your wife's lawyer if you win. If your wife's lawyer is a courthouse shark cruising the divorce waters just waiting for a fat fish like you to swim by, note the catatonic shock when it becomes clear that your wife will have to foot the bill and she only has $150.

Note: In many states, the husband still manages and controls the marriage property. In these states, there is a presumption that the husband is in a superior position to the wife in respect to property settlement negotiation. It is particularly important to be assured that your wife is represented by an attorney and that the agreement recite this representation. Otherwise, you may find yourself back in court defending yourself on a fraud or misrepresentation charge.

Negotiation: How, When, and Where

Dan wants a divorce, and so does his wife, Tina. They have been married eight years. Five years were relatively happy, two were tolerable, and the last was a disaster. Dan left several days ago. He called Tina yesterday and asked to speak with their two children. Tina yelled at him, cried, and finally hung up.

Leaving a marriage, even a destructive one, is a fearful proposition. Like Dan, your marriage probably was important to you even though things turned out badly. Both you and your wife are likely to feel upset about the failure of your marriage, and your focus will still be on this past relationship. You may talk of houses, bank accounts, and the like, but you may be much more concerned with your own anger, guilt, fear, helplessness, and loss. These are normal feelings; you need not berate yourself or your wife for feeling this way.

This, however, is *not* the time to negotiate anything permanent. You shared experiences, time, money, dreams, and perhaps children. You should allow yourself some time to mourn a dead marriage and see how your new life is shaping up.

Eventually you will find yourself getting bored with feeling mad, guilty, and lonely. You will have accepted that your marriage is over, and then you will start to want to get on with your life. This is a sign that you are ready to negotiate. Unfortunately, one of you may reach this point before the other. If this happens to you, try to allow your wife a reasonable amount of time — say up to six months — before forcing the settlement issue.

Knowing What You Want   It sounds kind of silly to say that you must know what you want in order to negotiate sensibly for a settlement agreement. But it isn't. To negotiate successfully you need to decide optimally what you want, what your priorities are, and what the minimum is that you can accept. Remember that in most states who was to blame for your separation is not relevant. The issues you may need to work out are:
- grounds for divorce in states where this is applicable
- child custody and visitation
- child and spousal support
- property (and debt) distribution

Each of these issues can affect the other. Concessions in one area may give you negotiating leverage in another.

If you have a child, think first about child custody. Once you decide this question, the other issues are likely to fall into place. Ask yourself the following questions and see how many you want to answer *in writing*: Am I *sure* that:
- I will or won't sacrifice a lot to spend time with my children?

- I enjoy feeding, clothing, and getting the kids to school as much as I enjoy reading to them?
- I will or won't sacrifice custody rights for money, up to a point?
- I will or won't sacrifice money for custody rights, up to a point?
- My own needs will not change after the divorce and that child custody may be an intrusion?
- My personal future is predictable enough for me to specify visitation rights?

Saying "no," or "I'm *not* sure" to all these questions does not mean you're Mr. Indecisive. It simply means that you're probably more honest than most people. Trying to project your own preferences and circumstances for the next 10 or 15 years is asking a lot of yourself.

Strategies for Negotiating   You can negotiate directly with your wife or through your attorneys. If you negotiate directly, you will save money on attorney's fees. However, even if you do this it is advisable in most cases to have an attorney draw up your actual agreement.

Before negotiating you should know:
- what you and your wife own separately and jointly
- what your debts are
- what your respective incomes and earning potentials are
- what the domestic relations law of your state provides
- what you want
- what your priorities are
- what is the minimum you will accept

We believe that the best goals for a marital settlement are to provide reasonably for the support and welfare of your children, to provide for a speedy and fair termination of your relationship, and to end your financial and emotional dependence on one another. With this in mind, it is often strategic to:
- concede to a good custody and support plan for your child
- concede property in order to avoid spousal support

- give your wife financial encouragement to become self-supporting (time-limited spousal support)
- avoid the responsibility of handling your ex-wife's financial affairs
- be flexible
- forget so-called "principles" and concede trivial items
- constantly remember your priorities and the minimum that you will accept

Be prepared to settle for something between what you think is fair and what is minimally acceptable. If you and your wife *both* feel that you have conceded more than is fair, then your agreement is probably reasonable.

Throughout the negotiations, it might be well to bear in mind that people have been known to act for reasons other than pure self-interest. Your wife may agree to more visitation than she wants because she feels it would be good for the kids. And you, on the other hand, may agree to pay more child support than the court would order because you want your children to have the best you can provide. And, believe it or not, some divorcing spouses will concede a point simply because they realize that it is important to the other partner, and that person's happiness is still important to them even though the relationship is ending.

However, spite, envy, disillusionment, and anger motivate many spouses even in settlement negotiations, where such feelings are generally self-destructive. You may have a fanatical wish to punish your ex-spouse, despite the cost to yourself. Or you may break off settlement negotiations because you *really want* a long, bitter custody fight — no matter what your attorney advises. If so, good luck. You'll need it. And you'll certainly pay for it.

When an Agreement May Be Made You may make a marital settlement agreement at any time before the judge issues the final judgment or decree of divorce. Obviously, the earlier you settle the divorce, the less you will pay in costs and attorney's fees. Settlements made in court (often under pressure from the judge hearing the matter) are expensive, since both attorneys have already finished all the pretrial

125

work and made appearances (which may cost up to $500 per day or more).

Most states have what are called "pretrial conferences," in which the attorneys for both sides sum up their contentions and define the issues. You will not be present at this conference but may be called in to approve a settlement offer that has been made. Whenever you are asked to approve a settlement on the advice of your attorney, take your time, and be sure you read carefully and understand clearly all the terms and conditions of the proposal and feel they are fair. Don't panic or approve a settlement because you're tired of the whole messy situation!

At some point in the court proceedings, if you get this far, the judge may indicate to the respective attorneys what the ruling will be if the matter proceeds. Needless to say, you must accommodate your demands to this reality — as must your wife.

Where and How Negotiations Are Conducted Settlement negotiations may be begun and completed without your ever seeing your wife. Or it may happen that you are forced into face-to-face encounters on numerous occasions. It all depends on how your respective attorneys handle marital settlements, what questions come up that are handled best by on-the-spot discussions, and how rational you and your wife are.

While there is no need for cozy chats every day, an immense amount of time and money can be saved if you are available for personal discussion with your wife at given times (with both attorneys present, of course). Endless telephone calls and letters setting forth positions and counter-positions are costly and time-consuming. In addition, you will constantly be bedeviled by the conviction that your wife couldn't *really* be insisting on this or that — it *has* to be that damned lawyer of hers! Personal confrontations can help clear up at least some of this nonsense.

Ordinarily, settlement negotiations are conducted in the office of either your attorney or your wife's. As long as you're well represented, don't bother very much about any supposed advantage she may gain by having them in her lawyer's office. If this makes her feel more at home or more secure — fine and good. Just don't be overwhelmed by her lawyer's original Van Goghs or fine walnut appointments. If you feel intimidated, you'll lose the feeling fast by remembering that some poor sucker helped pay for everything.

If your attorney does settlement business with you by telephone (which will probably happen), be sure to take notes of the substance of the conversations and keep them. Lawyers are busy. They are also careless and often lazy. They should be kept on their toes. At the end of a conversation, summarize the points decided or not decided, and ask your lawyer to verify your understanding of the conversation.

Property Division

The kinds of property involved in a marriage and each spouse's interest in them are defined in Chapter Ten. *Property*, as used in this section, refers chiefly to joint property accumulated during the marriage and includes personal and real property.

The following is a checklist of property and other related items that should be considered in every property settlement agreement:
- real property (land, houses, buildings)
- mortgages, trust deeds, or leases
- option rights (given or received)
- bank accounts, safe-deposit boxes
- cash on hand
- insurance
- receivables (loans, deferred salary, royalties, promissory notes, and the like)
- stocks and other securities
- pensions, profit-sharing plans, annuities
- personal property
- business interests
- income

- miscellaneous assets (tax-loss carryforwards, club memberships, trusts, copyrights, and so on)
- liabilities
- any pending lawsuits or judgments
- gifts made to wife by you or by wife to you

Don't Conceal Your Assets Many married persons are surprised to discover how little they know about their partner's earnings or assets. Some men keep their wives in complete ignorance of their finances, while others completely turn over management of the family assets to their wives.

You may be tempted to conceal your assets from your wife in settlement negotiations. This is a bad idea on any number of counts, particularly when your wife is represented by a good attorney. Some of the consequences of concealing assets may be prosecution for perjury (the agreement states that each party swears under penalty of perjury that he or she has not concealed assets), a civil action for fraud, and an action to set aside (negate) the agreement.

Each attorney has a duty to tell his or her client not to conceal assets. But even if yours doesn't mention it, disclose your income and assets — it's money in the bank.

Verification of the Income and Assets of Your Partner Perhaps your wife claims that your income is more than you have revealed in the papers you've filled out in connection with the divorce. Or perhaps you suspect that your wife's income is greater than she has admitted.

There are various methods to establish each person's true income and assets, including depositions (questions and answers made under oath) and investigative services. On a more practical level, however, this information may be approximated by an examination of the items involved in your mutual standard of living and the cost of these items. In most cases, the expenditures are paid for by check (which of course is proof of the amount). Where items are paid for by cash, estimates will have to be made.

Following is a checklist of the items involved in a couple's

standard of living that may often be examined to determine income or assets:
- the home and what it costs to maintain it
- the cost of running and feeding the family
- automobile costs
- medical and dental costs
- vacations and entertainment
- clothing
- education costs
- miscellaneous costs

Tax Returns   Federal and state tax returns are often indispensable in negotiating a fair marital settlement. Although they cannot be taken at face value, for purposes of divorce, nevertheless, they may normally be used to establish income, debts that carry interest, investments, and so on. If your wife has the returns for the years you need and she will not relinquish them to you (or your lawyer), your lawyer can usually obtain them through a court order. If an accountant prepared the returns for you, copies will usually be given to you. Or, if you wish, call the IRS Service Center nearest you, tell them to send you IRS Form No. 4506, fill it in, sign it, and return it. This method usually takes about two or three months, however.

Proper use of the tax returns is, of course, up to your attorney. Remember, however, that if you had an extraordinarily high income in recent tax years and have averaged income, your wife's attorney should be made aware of this.

If your wife tries to obtain the tax returns of a business in which you are a partner (or a stockholder in a closely held corporation), prepare your firm's accountant ahead of time. You should have the accountant verify business expenses that your wife may claim are part of your income (such as entertainment expenses and travel and depreciation). Your accountant should be able to produce proof, if necessary, that these expenses are not exaggerated.

Handling Depositions   If your attorney is thorough and there are unanswered questions regarding your wife's circumstances, a number of legal tools are available to gain information from her. These tools are called "discovery." And, of course, they can be used by your wife's attorney to gain information from you.

These tools include written questions that must be answered under oath, depositions (oral questions and answers under oath, recorded by a court reporter in most instances), subpoenas that are directed to documents, and the like.

If you are on the receiving end of these procedures, your attorney will advise you how to handle them. Follow this advice! If you don't, you can really damage your case and ruin your negotiating position. Some of the questions may be personal and may offend you or seem far-fetched. Never mind. Your attorney's job is to instruct you to answer those questions that are *legally* proper and relevant and to prevent you from answering those that are inadmissible in court or are too wide off the mark. Keep your temper and respond as best you can. Remember that your wife's attorney will be evaluating you as a potential witness, speculating on how you'll handle yourself on the stand. If you do well, you will greatly improve your bargaining position for settlement.

Do You Need an Accountant?   If large income and substantial assets are involved in your divorce, you or your wife may need the services of a certified public accountant or a public accountant. If this is the case, it will be helpful if you can both agree on who to hire. Your respective attorneys may be of assistance in this respect. If you can't agree, it may be necessary for each of you to hire your own.

Do You Need a Tax Expert?   One very important factor that you must consider in negotiating a separation agreement with your wife is the implication of the agreement for your tax situation. People contemplating divorce are often overwhelmed by reference to taxes and tax terminology.

You should retain a tax expert if the property involved in your divorce settlement is substantial. A tax expert's suggestions on the contents of a marital settlement agreement are more than worth the cost in practically every case.

Debts and Payment of Debts

The agreement should include a list of all obligations for which either or both of you are personally liable. The list should include all obligations that are payable only in the future, as well as any that are contingent (payment for services yet to be performed, possible recovery of lawsuit damages, and so on).

You may find it helpful to separate debts that are secured, such as the mortgage on your home. Where appropriate, it is also helpful to indicate, opposite each debt, whether or not your joint property or the separate property of either of you is liable for the debt (if unpaid).

A checklist of information regarding each debt listed follows:

- the name and address of the creditor
- the date incurred and the present amount outstanding
- a payment schedule and the rate of interest
- whether the payment is current (if not, the amount of delinquent payments plus penalties)
- whether the debt is set forth in a document (promissory note, mortgage, credit card statement, and so on)
- whether the debt is secured
- whether any co-signers or guarantors exist on the debt

The agreement should specify how and when payment of the debts is to be made. Payment may be arranged, for example, by either or both persons, from a community obligation special account, or from the sale of assets.

If the debt is the separate obligation of one of the spouses, the agreement should provide for payment by the liable spouse.

Remember in this connection that one or the other of you may find it convenient or financially beneficial to personally assume more than your share of the community debts in exchange for a concession elsewhere. For example:

Jim is in a high tax bracket and needs all the deductions he can get under the agreement. He agrees to pay more spousal support than reasonable and to assume more than his share of the community debts in exchange for a greater share of the joint property. This bargain will lower his tax liability.

Flexibility in Negotiations

Remember when negotiating property settlements that all the marital property (and income) should be examined, together with all the community debts. In the absence of spousal or child support, it should be fairly easy for you and your wife to distribute the property equitably to suit each of your needs. For example:

Dave, Jeanne, and the bank own a house worth $65,000. $37,000 is still owing on the house, and the payments are $341 a month. Jeanne inherited $18,000, which was used as a down payment. Dave has worked all eight years of their marriage and as a result has $11,000 in a pension fund and $5,000 in annuities. Jeanne worked two years of their marriage and has $2,100 in a pension fund and $1,200 in annuities. They own two cars, one worth slightly more than the other. Their home is full of slightly worn furniture that they still owe $3,000 on. Dave and Jeanne agree to distribute the property as follows: Jeanne gets the house and the furniture. Each will keep their individual pension and annuity benefits. Dave will assume the $3,000 debt and will take the better of the two cars.

Spousal Support and Maintenance

If you're a typical husband and father, you'll find agreeing to a reasonable amount for child support easier than agreeing to spousal support. The former, you may feel, helps your child, while the latter helps your ex-wife. This feeling is illusory, however, and you may as well rid yourself of it.

For one thing, the chances are good that you'll be paying both support obligations in a single check. Second, any benefits that go to the child (such as good housing, excellent food, and entertainment expenses) will also go to your former wife. As the custodial parent, she will share almost any benefit you provide for the child except, perhaps, educational benefits later on. In any event, do your best to make or agree to make support payments — whether to your wife or child — on a factual basis.

There are a number of important reasons why a support agreement should be fair to both husband and wife — apart from the legal considerations. First, if the agreement is fair it will probably *work* and save you and your wife time and money (not to mention emotional stress) further down the road. If the agreement is unfair to either of you, the person affected will find a way to protest or avoid complying with the agreement, in court or out of court.

Amount of Support

Joe is a teacher and earns $20,000 a year plus fringe benefits. Connie is a former teacher who now believes that teaching will offer her few opportunities in the future. She wants to get into the personnel field and has taken night school classes with this goal in mind. Joe has agreed to pay Connie spousal support of $400 a month for the two years required to finish her educational program. By this time the children will both be in school. Joe will also pay $200 child support for each child. The children and Connie will continue to receive medical and dental insurance through Joe's coverage at work.

There is no fixed mathematical formula for determining fair spousal support; nor, if the husband is to pay support, can a fixed percentage of his income be used. For example, if you make $12,000 a year, 30 percent of your net income may be insufficient to support your wife. On the other hand, if you make $1,000,000 a year, the same percentage may be more than enough.

Generally the amount agreed on for support should be sufficient for the reasonable needs of the spouse receiving it and fair to the spouse paying it, considering his or her means.

In negotiating support in settlement proceedings, more or less the same guidelines employed by a judge in determining support should be used. The following, at least, must be considered:

- How much does the spouse who is to receive support reasonably need?
- Will the support proposed allow the person receiving it to maintain an adequate standard of living that is roughly comparable to that of the person paying it?
- How much can the person paying support reasonably afford?
- What is his or her income?
- Is it steady or does it fluctuate?
- What are the person's future prospects?

- Has the other person made non-monetary contributions?
- What assets does each party own?
- Has either party built up the other's assets by monetary or other contributions?
- Does either party have separate, independent income? If so, how much?
- What are the reasonable expectations of the supported spouse as regards earning income?
- How far in the future will this occur?
- Does he or she have the necessary experience and preparation?

Expected Changes in Wife's Future Income

Lisa has not worked in six years even though she is a trained bookkeeper capable of earning an excellent salary. Ken, her husband, offers her $600 a month spousal support for six months, and $200 a month for the following year.

Your wife's income will, in all probability, fluctuate. If so, you will want to adjust any maintenance payments you promise to her, while giving her a continuing incentive to work and improve her income.

An adjustment can be agreed on that simply reflects the percentage changes in her income. Remember in this connection that spousal support agreements almost always contain a provision for automatic cost of living increases, based on the consumer price index (Bureau of Labor Statistics). Any adjustment will have to take into account this built-in change.

Expected Changes in Your Income If your wife thinks you are on the brink of financial success, she (or her lawyer) will probably demand that the agreement provide for adjustments as your income increases. Be advised that the courts have generally refused to order support under a formula that automatically entitles the wife to share (proportionately) in any increases in her husband's income. In fact, judges have pointed out that such an arrangement, without regard to the possible increases in the husband's financial burden, might represent a hardship on the husband.

There may be some instances, however, where you would be willing to accept such a provision if you gained some other advantage that was important to you. If this is the case, the agreement should provide some adequate method to determine your income in future years in order to avoid recurring problems. You might want your accountant to help with this provision, rather than agreeing to produce your tax returns after the divorce.

Lump-Sum or Time Payments?

Nick and his lawyer appraise his situation and believe that he will be required to pay spousal support of about $300 a month for the next four years. This translates into $14,000 total. Nick does not want to be bothered with spousal support or future contact with his ex-wife. He offers to give her his interest in the family home, about $12,000, if she will waive spousal support.

In negotiating agreement on support payments of any kind, but particularly spousal support, the relative advantages and disadvantages of lump-sum payment or payment over a period of time may be crucial. ("Lump-sum" as used here includes the transfer of money or property.)

Advantages Depending, of course, on her financial circumstances, your wife may have several reasons for preferring a lump sum in partial or complete satisfaction of an agreed-on amount for support. The first, of course, is inflation — a dollar received today promises to be worth more than a dollar received a year from now. Second, the money or property she receives now can be invested or reinvested. Third, there is always a chance that part of the obligation may be difficult or impossible for her to collect later on.

Some of the advantages to you in a lump-sum payment may be the reduced risk of having the support modified later, the fact that at one stroke you have fulfilled your obligation and need not worry about writing out monthly checks, the elimination of the necessity of transacting business with your wife if that promises to be difficult, and possibly certain tax advantages.

Disadvantages There are also disadvantages to be considered. First, you probably cannot deduct the lump-sum payment for income tax purposes. Second, in some states a lump-sum settlement is not completely conclusive and your wife later may request support if the payment has been squandered or lost.

If you feel strongly about not making a lump-sum payment, or are unable to do so, you may be able to negotiate something in-between that will be acceptable to your wife. For example:

David and Angela plan to divorce; they own only a coin collection appraised at $20,000. Their property is to be equally divided. David wants to keep and maintain the collection but doesn't have $10,000 to pay Angela her half. He proposes that he pay her $4,000 per year for the next three years for her interest.

In this example, Angela is being compensated $2,000 extra for any risk she is taking or the disadvantage in not having the money in hand.

Recommendation: A Trust If you want some of the advantages of a lump-sum method and want to avoid some of the disadvantages, ask your attorney about setting up an irrevocable trust. Such a trust may provide sufficient income for the agreed-on needs of your wife and children and is subject to none of the problems that may arise from periodic payments or a lump-sum payment.

Cost of Medical Care Men are often required to meet the medical and dental expenses of their ex-spouses and children. This is an extremely open-ended and ambiguous expense. Does it mean $50-an-hour therapy sessions for your wife and $3,800 worth of cosmetic orthodonture for your child? We suggest that you offer to carry insurance coverage for your wife and children if this is an issue.

Effect of Bankruptcy, Death, or Remarriage Under the federal bankruptcy law, a discharge in bankruptcy releases you from almost all debts *except wife or child support*.

Payments made under an agreement stop at the death of

the person making them unless the agreement provides otherwise.

Also unless the agreement provides otherwise, any payments made by you to your wife stop when she remarries. The same rule is true when you remarry, if you receive support.

Note: Some men include a provision for spousal support to continue in a reduced amount for a relatively short time after their former wife remarries. These men feel that such a provision can help induce their former wife to remarry, whereas large support payments that cease at marriage act as a deterrent to her remarriage. Note further, though, that the courts do not consider living with someone else as being remarried. If you make this type of provision, be prepared to accept the possibility that your former wife may be collecting support and living with another man.

Child Custody, Support, and Visitation

Before reading this section, you might want to read Chapters Eleven through Fourteen, dealing with custody and the rules for determining it.

A custody agreement should specify the names of the children, where they will reside, their birthdates and ages, past addresses, the place of education, and the name of the custodial parent.

If the agreement is for joint custody, in addition to the above, it should specify the custodial parents, the times and places their custody will be exercised, and any relevant provisions concerning support.

A custody agreement, in order to work, must be in the best interests of your child and it must be fair to you and your wife. As is true with child support, any agreement on custody that you and your wife make is *not conclusive* in court. If the agreement doesn't work, either of you can later go back into court and request that the arrangement be changed — no matter what the agreement provides.

Obviously, both you and your wife must give some consideration to who would be awarded custody if it came to a court trial. Your attorney should be able to give you an educated guess on this.

If your wife is to be given custody of the children, you should demand to have some voice in their future. You might, if you wish, provide for mutual consultation with your wife on the children's education, health, religious training, vacations, and the like. True, this will offer another chance for you and your wife to fight, if that's your preference, but it also affords you a chance to participate actively in your children's future.

If appropriate, you should negotiate for a change of custody when the children reach a certain age. You should also negotiate a provision, if appropriate, that if your wife remarries the children are to carry your name, unless you give express permission otherwise or unless the children are legally adopted.

As far as visitation is concerned, the custody agreement should provide that child support payments are suspended during the visitation period (if it is an extended one).

Here is a checklist of matters to be considered when making a custody agreement:

- which parent is to have custody
- what visitation is allowed the non-custodial spouse, including the circumstances, frequency, how much advance notice, and specification of the suspension of child support payments
- a statement that the custodial parent may or may not remove the child from a given area without the permission of the non-custodial parent
- who is to pay traveling expenses, if travel is involved, including a determination of when it is necessary for someone to accompany the child
- the consequences of the frustration of visitation rights, including arbitration, court orders, and the cessation of spousal support
- the respective rights of the parents to make decisions affecting the child's future
- the termination of custody, including whether it should be before the child becomes of age

• the name that the child is to carry, covering the remarriage of the custodial parent and the death of the noncustodial parent

How It Can Work — An Example

Herb and Marcie have a six-year-old son and a four-year-old daughter. Since their son's birth, Marcie has stayed home with the children. A year ago, when it was obvious that their marriage was shaky, Marcie thought she'd better develop some independent resources and started going to night school. As a result, Herb became more involved with and closer to the children. Herb and Marcie agree that Marcie should have custody of the children; however, visitation will be liberal. Herb will continue to care for the children while Marcie is at night school, and he will have the children two weekends a month and for a month-and-a-half during the summer.

Technical Requirements of the Agreement

Each state has its own requirements governing the form of marital settlement agreements, how they must be signed and notarized, and where and when they are to be filed. Similarly, the procedure for obtaining the judge's approval of the agreement varies from state to state.

In general, the agreement should be in writing and, if it affects real property, it must comply with any state law governing such contracts. The agreement must be signed and dated by both parties and their attorneys. Most states require the agreement to be acknowledged (before witnesses) or notarized. It is then filed in the court where the divorce is pending for the judge's approval. If the judge does not approve, then it's back to square one. If it's approved, the agreement is incorporated into the final judgment or decree of divorce.

Can the Agreement Be Changed Later? You and your wife have the power to change the agreement you made, provided that your children are properly protected. In most cases, though, changes will be difficult, since property has in all likelihood changed hands, money has been paid, and so on. Still, you are now legally strangers and just like anyone else you have the right to contract if you wish.

The court that issued the divorce decree, after approving the agreement, can change the agreement under certain conditions. First, if the provisions for support are separable from the property provisions, the support provisions may be modified later (increased or decreased). In other words, the agreement is not integrated. Second, a judge can change the support provisions later if the agreement itself authorizes such a change.

A marital settlement agreement cannot be modified if it is integrated. For example:

Alex agreed to give Anna his share of the house in exchange for her promise to accept $50 per month as support. The agreement is integrated and Anna may not later request that her support be changed.

Remember that child support is always subject to change by the court, provided the circumstances dictate. You and your wife simply cannot make an agreement that unalterably fixes your respective rights as regards child support.

Reconciliation Your agreement should provide that if you reconcile with your wife, the agreement is still binding. This will help protect you against the possible consequences of a reconciliation, such as clouding the title to property received in the settlement. Furthermore, if you or your wife have the right to receive future payments under the agreement or if either will assume debts in exchange for certain property given up, the result would obviously be unfair.

If you and your wife do reconcile and you want to cancel the agreement, simply draw up another contract that nullifies the effects of the first one.

9
Spousal Support

*It's the end of the month, the bills are due, and Frank and Ellen
settle in for their usual fight. Both work, their young child is relegated
to a day-care mother, and still they are barely able to meet their
expenses. No chance of saving for a house, no new furniture, and
no vacation this year. Frank must first meet his support obligations
to the woman he divorced five years ago.*

Spousal support (alimony) is a hated reality for many men.
It is a periodic reminder of a relationship that failed — a
vehicle for continued contact and disagreement with a
divorced spouse. It intrudes financially and emotionally into
a man's new life, and it never allows him to be completely
free of the woman from whom he separated.

The subject of spousal support is irksome from both a
legal and a practical viewpoint — legally, since it is questionable whether marriage should entitle anyone to a lifetime
of financial protection, and practically, since there is seldom
enough money to be fair to both parties.

Spousal Support and Alimony:
Changing Purposes

Alimony is now an archaic term — a survivor from the days
when marriage was both a permanent arrangement and a
woman's primary career. Women who behaved themselves
were entitled to a lifelong meal ticket. The rules were simple:
Don't desert the home, don't commit adultery, and don't

commit a moral outrage. Women who broke the rules were left out in the cold financially; men who broke the rules paid alimony.

For some time this system has not reflected the new realities of working, self-sufficient wives and widespread divorce. The concept of spousal support represents an attempt by the lawmakers to modernize alimony. The fault of either the husband or wife is often no longer the issue: a person receives spousal support because of *need*, not because he or she has been sinned against. Theoretically, spousal support is paid to a former partner in order to compensate for non-monetary contributions to a marriage, provide job retraining, or maintain an ex-partner who is unable to work.

This change has corrected some of the more flagrant abuses of alimony. However, many states still have laws that consider the misdeeds of a husband or wife in awarding spousal support. And in practice, spousal support is almost always the man's burden. For every female bank president who supports her quadriplegic ex-husband, there are thousands of average men who support their former wives.

Spousal Support as a Form of Discrimination Against Men

Traditionally, spousal support was a duty imposed only on the husband. The rationale for this was that wives were homemakers and mothers who devoted their energies and skills to the maintenance of the family and, if deprived of maintenance by their husbands, would be unable to maintain themselves (and their children) decently.

To a great extent this was good reasoning. Few men would argue that a wife who has devoted twenty years to her marriage, often on demand of her husband, should, on the whim of her husband, be tossed out of house and home and be left to fend for herself. However, alimony was often regarded as a penalty for the husband's "sins": if you play, you pay.

Before March 1979 the laws of many states provided that

only women or "handicapped," "dependent," or "needy" men could receive spousal support. However, the United States Supreme Court then decided that state laws restricting spousal support to wives only were unconstitutional, since they violated the equal protection clause of the federal constitution. The Court stated:

[The] old notion that generally it is the man's primary responsibility to provide a home and its essentials no longer justifies laws that discriminate on the basis of sex.
[Orr vs. Orr, S Ct., March, 1979]

All states with outdated laws were required to change them, and most have, although some still have not. Whether your state has changed its laws or not, rest assured that you have the same right to spousal support as your wife.

Agreement or Court Order?

Agreement We *strongly* urge that if at all possible you work out a spousal support agreement with your wife, rather than take your chances in court. There are many reasons for this, but perhaps the most important are: (1) there are ten or more plans under which spousal support may be paid, and you may be able to tailor one to your specific needs; (2) there are alternatives to spousal support in the traditional form, such as spousal support "trusts" and the like; and (3) the tax advantages may be immense.

Court Order First, you should be aware that in most divorce cases coming before the courts these days spousal support is not ordered for either partner. This is hardly surprising in view of the economic makeup of most younger couples today, in which each partner makes a similar financial contribution.

Court orders for spousal support are of two kinds: *temporary support,* which is intended to maintain a spouse during the court proceedings; and *permanent support,* which continues until the end of a specified period.

The judge hearing the divorce usually makes the support order. He or she may, depending on the circumstances, order that the support be paid in money — either in periodic payments or in a lump sum — or that property be transferred in lieu of money (in Pennsylvania and Texas, for example).

Note: In many states support orders include a limit on the number of years they will run.

Amount of Support

New law now requires judges to award spousal support on the basis of need to either husband or wife. Should you and your wife be unable to agree about spousal support, what factors will a judge consider in making an award?

Criteria   Many states (about thirty-five) have specific laws that enumerate the factors a judge must consider in awarding spousal support to one of the spouses. But even those states without specific laws generally use the same criteria, which are:
  • the earning capacity and needs of each person
  • the debts and assets, including the separate property, of each person
  • how long the marriage lasted
  • marital misconduct (in some states only)
  • the ability of the supported person to obtain gainful employment without interfering with the legitimate interests of dependent children in his or her custody
  • how long it might take for the supported spouse to acquire appropriate education, training, and employment
  • the age and health of the persons
  • the standard of living of the persons
  • non-monetary contributions to the marriage community, such as services as a homemaker, assisting the career of the spouse, parenting, and contributing to the well-being of the family
  • any other factors the judge feels are fair and reasonable
  Note: In some instances, the judge will also consider a pre-

nuptial agreement if the parties have made one but cannot agree on whether it should be enforced.

Each support case is of course decided on the basis of its own facts and circumstances, regardless of which criteria are used. Consider the following cases:

Kathy, aged 27, is a star management trainee at a bank. Her marriage has been less successful. After two years together — no savings, no debts, and no children — she and her husband plan to go their separate ways.

Janice, aged 38, worked as a teacher until she was 30. At that time, she and her husband agreed that she should leave her job and take care of their first baby. She and her husband have now mutually decided to end their marriage.

Edna, aged 56, devoted her energies to rearing a family and being a homemaker. She bakes fine bread but has not finished high school, has never held a job, and has no pension or social security rights. Max, her husband of 40 years, wants a divorce.

A marriage license is not a ticket to a perpetual pension. Kathy did not sacrifice her career during her brief marriage and obviously is capable of continuing her life without the financial help of her former husband. Janice, the ex-teacher, disrupted her career with her husband's agreement. She may need financial assistance while she is training for the current job market and until she is able to re-establish her earning power. On the other hand, 56-year-old Edna may never be able to support herself adequately.

If the parties agreed that the woman was to be the home-maker, if the marriage lasts for a long period, and if the wife is unemployable when the couple separates, the husband simply has to accept the fact that his support responsibilities are going to last a long time — perhaps for life. This has nothing to do with feminism, sexism, male chauvinism, or any other fashionable ideology. It is simply common sense, basic decency, and ordinary justice.

Marital Misconduct

Sally is among the numerous other Californians who enjoy the relaxation of a soak in a hot tub. Unfortunately she generously shared the favors of her tub and, as a result, was divorced by her husband. Sally's frolics in the water have no effect on the amount of spousal

support she will receive. Her ex-husband, sadly a Californian, may be the one who gets "soaked."
Dick, a tourist from Connecticut, was one of Sally's tubmates. His wife found out and sued him for divorce. Dick can expect a second soaking. In Connecticut, Dick's misdeeds in the tub may affect the amount of spousal support he is required to pay.

Sally lives in one of the growing number of states that no longer consider who is at fault when granting divorce or awarding support.

These states are — in addition to California — Alaska, Arizona, Colorado, Delaware, Hawaii, Illinois, Minnesota, Montana, Ohio, Oregon, South Dakota, and Washington.

Dick, on the other hand, is a resident of a state that still bases divorce — and to some extent spousal support — on the idea of fault (marital misconduct). In the great majority of instances, the marital misconduct referred to is adultery. These states are — in addition to Connecticut — Georgia, Louisiana, North Carolina, Rhode Island, South Carolina, Tennessee, Virginia, and West Virginia.

The trend, though, is definitely away from using fault as an important factor in awarding spousal support. We feel that this is as it should be, since spousal support should be based on the needs and circumstances of the parties and should not be exacted as a penalty.

Economic Misconduct

Claudette accompanied her husband to New York for a convention. Before she left, she withdrew the family savings and lost it all at a New York racetrack.

A growing number of states provide that the economic misconduct of either husband or wife can be considered in making a spousal support award. In this context, *economic misconduct* means harming or dissipating the economic resources of the marriage without justification. Currently, states making this provision include Arizona, Delaware, District of Columbia, Hawaii, Indiana, Illinois, and Montana.

Displaced Homemakers: Non-Monetary Contributions

*Thirty years ago Adele left a promising career as a ballet dancer
to marry Roscoe. Since then she has selflessly devoted herself to her
husband and her children. Adele, now 52, is still a nice woman.
But she is 50 pounds heavier, unattractive, uneducated, and boring.
Roscoe has decided to spend his remaining years with a beautiful
young jazz dancer.*

Whenever the foes of alimony become too vocal, the poor
Adeles are mentioned. And we all know them. They are those
unfortunate women who have always been homemakers and
in their middle years find themselves "displaced" by
divorce. Besides their obvious lack of job skills, these women
are discriminated against on the basis of age, and are in-
eligible for pension, welfare, health, and other benefits.

As a result of these problems, "displaced homemaker"
laws have been enacted in a number of states. In a sense,
there is nothing new in the concept — judges have always
taken into consideration non-monetary contributions to the
marriage by one of the spouses in making spousal support
orders. What *is* new, though, is that various states have now
tried to give this factor specific recognition in their laws;
that is, they have taken what was once a bundle of circumstances (hard to pin down and evaluate) and given them
specific form and substance in the law. The result is usually
called the "displaced homemaker" law.

The states that have enacted such laws are:

California	Kentucky	Montana
Colorado	Maine	Nebraska
Delaware	Maryland	New Hampshire
District of	Massachusetts	Ohio
Columbia	Michigan	Oregon
Florida	Minnesota	Rhode Island
Illinois	Mississippi	Virginia
Indiana	Missouri	Wisconsin

Obviously, these laws were enacted primarily to benefit
women. They are intended to require ex-husbands to provide
support until their ex-wives acquire job skills or become
eligible for social security or pension benefits.

Men should note, however, that many states provide

147

extensive counseling and training programs for displaced homemakers. Ex-wives with a reasonable degree of intelligence, health, and sanity should be expected to use these programs and after a period of time become responsible for their own support.

Helping Your Spouse through School Other non-monetary matters are frequently considered by judges in making spousal support orders. One of the most common of these is assisting one's spouse to complete his or her education — usually at some sacrifice to the person rendering the assistance.

As in the following case, it is usually women who are compensated for supporting their ex-husbands while they were going to school.

At the time of separation, Eleanor was in her twenties, in good health, and able to support herself. There were no children. Eleanor and Jim were living in Nebraska. Over the objection of her husband, Eleanor was awarded spousal support of $6,500, payable at $100 a month for five-and-one-half years. The basis for the judge's ruling that she had worked to support her husband while he studied and obtained his degree.

Remember, however, that the law can work both ways. These days women often continue or finish their education while their husbands support them. In these situations, men may be entitled to spousal support. Consider the following:

Alvin, who had always wanted to be an engineer, worked as a carpenter in order to support his family. When their children were grown, Hattie, his wife, went back to college. Alvin continued working. Hattie became a lawyer and sued Alvin for divorce. Alvin now demands that Hattie support him through engineering school.

Effects of Child Support Awards Spousal support and child support orders are separate and distinct matters and are treated separately by the law — or should be — even though they are often in the same judgment.

Still, some judges notoriously tend to use one order or the other to penalize a spouse when restricted by law from awarding more than is reasonable in a given case.

Pete's wife divorces him after discovering his longstanding relationship with another woman. She requests child and spousal support. The judge can order only $200 a month per child under the law. But to teach Pete a lesson, he orders Pete to pay $800 per month spousal support, which is unreasonable under the circumstances. Pete should appeal the judge's order.

Conversely, of course, if a judge is restricted in the amount of spousal support that can be ordered, the child support order may — not unreasonably — be made to compensate for the judge's moral outrage.

The Ability of the Spouse to Become Self-Supporting

A growing number of judges focus on the ability of the spouse receiving support to become self-supporting. Support will be ordered to give the spouse time to make a transition to a new life, but only for a limited period to prevent an able-bodied person from living off the labors of an ex-spouse.

This is one of the most obvious reasons why, if you will be paying support, you should attempt to limit the length of the obligation. (In many states the length is limited by law.) Also remember in this connection that support awards under displaced homemaker laws usually set limits on the duration of support.

Here are some examples that illustrate these general principles:

In Arizona, a wife was awarded support of $400 per month for six months. The marriage had lasted fifteen months; the wife was forty-seven years old. Although her secretarial skills had been lost to some extent, she was in good mental and physical condition, was taking schooling to regain her skills, and was expected to be employed.

Remember, of course, that such examples assume no children who require a wife's presence at home.

Again in Arizona, a declining support order ($400 a month for 13 years and $200 a month for the last 2) was awarded to a wife until her youngest child was of age. The marriage had lasted about 4 years. The husband pointed out that his wife had a graduate degree and could earn over $18,000 a year. The judge replied that her earnings were speculative, but in any event she wanted to stay home with the children.

On occasions, judges simply seem to ignore all the principles mentioned above. For example:

In Seattle, a wife was awarded $175 a month for one year (1974), plus half of her husband's net earnings for ten years, following a six-year marriage. She was able-bodied, 46 years of age, and a competent stenographic employee.

Standard of Living   This has been one of the great catchalls of the spousal support law. Often it is used simply to "compensate" a woman for having lived with a man. Most frequently, of course, the standard of living factor has been employed where the divorcing husband is a celebrity, a notorious playboy, and the like. The following examples are fairly mild compared to some that have hit the headlines recently.

In South Carolina, a wife was awarded $150,000 in support (a lump sum) after a marriage of a little over a year. The husband, who was retired, was worth over four million dollars. The wife was relatively young, in good health, and capable of self-support. The judge mentioned, in passing, the wife's accustomed standard of living and the great differences in the parties' wealth.

In an eastern seaboard case, permanent support of $1,850 a month for twenty years was awarded to the wife of an entertainer, after two years of marriage. The wife, a musician, was employable, the couple had no children, and she had considerable separate property. The award was made on the basis of the standard of living she had enjoyed for the two years.

In practice, the "accustomed standard of living" gives way to the reality of the situation. Most judges accept the fact that the supporting spouse must have enough money to live on. Generally, a judge will try to find out what the supporting spouse needs in order to survive and to continue working. Then he or she will order the balance of the income distributed to the other spouse, the children, and the attorneys.

If you are ordered to pay support, your wife will probably be outraged when she discovers that she will not receive enough money from you to live as she has been living. She may be particularly outraged if your conduct has "caused" the divorce. Nevertheless, she must live with the order and you must be able to continue existing to pay it.

Serious Financial Loss by Husband or Wife   If a spouse
has suffered a significant financial loss due to her marriage,
an attorney can make a strong case for compensation:

*In California, a wife was the beneficiary of a trust created by her
deceased first husband (before her marriage), which paid her $516
monthly until her death or remarriage. At the end of a two-year
marriage, the judge decided that the husband was aware of these facts
when he married her and had accepted his responsibility to support
her. The judge awarded the wife full compensation for her loss, as well
as ordering $500 per month spousal support.*

On the other hand, judges have also decided the reverse:

*In South Dakota, a couple divorced after two-and-a-half years
of marriage. The wife had lost her social security benefits by marrying.
The judge rejected her claim that she was entitled to permanent support
but did award her $100 a month for one year. The judge stated that
while it was a fact that she had voluntarily relinquished her right
to payment of social security and other benefits on marriage, this fact
alone did not obligate her husband to compensate her for that loss.*

As may be evident, the courts are divided on the question
of who should bear the responsibility for financial loss due
to divorce.

Strategies

Spousal support is generally a long-term, costly, and disagreeable obligation. But you should not, through guilt or a
desire to be free of the inconvenience, agree to pay an outrageous amount of support. Nor should you try to avoid your
obligations to a penniless, unemployable ex-wife. However,
you must protect yourself.

There are many different ways of meeting a spousal support obligation. And, there are legitimate and fair ways to
avoid it. Discuss this with your attorney and consider your
various choices. Do this *before* making any agreement or
going to court.

Spousal support is often an excellent, fair, and expedient
way for a man to leave a relationship. Generally, though,
we believe that it is to a man's advantage not to meet his
obligations through periodic spousal support. When this is

151

impossible, we recommend that men try to limit the time for which support payments are required. Some of the reasons to avoid paying periodic spousal support are:

- You will hate paying it; each month you will be reminded that a portion of your income cannot be spent on a vacation, your new spouse, your own expenses, and so on.
- You will remain in contact with your ex-spouse.
- Should you be unable to pay, you must return to court and ask for a change. Failure to do so might result in your wages being attached.
- Should your income increase, you may be required to pay more.
- Should your ex-wife's health, income, or ability to support herself worsen, you may be required to pay more.

Marital Settlement Agreements   As we mentioned earlier, you should try to resolve the spousal support issue by agreement rather than by having a settlement imposed on you by the court. This is likely to save you and your ex-wife money and headaches.

Lump Sum Payments   Often it is advantageous to meet a spousal support obligation by giving a spouse all or a portion of your own separate property or a large share of the assets accumulated during a marriage, or by deeding your spouse the family home. By doing this you may be able to terminate your responsibilities permanently. This is generally accomplished by a marital settlement agreement.

High Support for a Short Time   High but short-lived spousal support provides your ex-wife with the incentive and the means to become self-supporting. In effect, you give her a limited period in which she is free from financial pressure, which gives her the opportunity to improve her employment skills and prospects.

Often this requires a man to live near the poverty level for several years. But it is only a determinate sentence. In the end, he can be free from legal obligations and, surely, residual guilt.

Avoid Token Spousal Support Frequently ex-wives ask for token support. Since a dollar a year is unlikely to hurt even the thinnest of budgets, men often comply with this request.

But, be warned: Any time the court makes a support order it can modify that order. This means that should you suddenly become rich (even relatively), your ex-wife can claim a share of your good fortune.

Tax Considerations You do *not* pay income taxes on spousal support that you furnish an ex-spouse; this support is deductible from your gross income. Your ex-wife, however, will pay income taxes on the support she receives.

Following your divorce your ex-wife's income bracket may be very low, and thus she may be in a better tax position than you. By paying relatively high spousal support for a short time, you may save yourself and her some money. This and other tax considerations are discussed in greater detail in Chapter Fourteen.

When Does Spousal Support Stop?

Obviously, the death of the person to whom you pay spousal support terminates your obligation, and the laws of many states limit the number of years a former spouse is obligated to pay spousal support. A seven-year maximum is typical. The rest of this discussion assumes that the state you live in has no such law.

If you and your ex-partner have agreed on a fixed amount of support, obviously it will last according to the terms of the agreement. If a judge has ordered support, the party may be ordered to furnish it for as long as the judge believes is just and reasonable. Remember always that as circumstances change, either you or your ex-partner may come back to court and apply for a change in the amount or duration of the order.

What If Your Supported Spouse Is Living with Someone?

Harry was ordered to pay his wife $250 a month support for seven years, based on the earning capacities of himself and his wife, their needs, and so on. One year later, Harry's wife moved in with Tom, who now foots most of the household bills. Harry, pretty ticked off, asks the court to stop or reduce his support payments.

Harry may or may not have his request granted. Only one state (Alabama) has a specific law providing that spousal support ceases when the person receiving it lives with another adult.

In New York, the mere fact that your former wife now lives with someone else does not necessarily entitle you to stop alimony payments, unless she has lived with the other person for at least six months and has held herself out as his wife. And in California, if your former wife now lives with someone else the court is authorized to modify the spousal support payments under which you may be obligated.

In other states, however, judges have terminated spousal support under such circumstances — not because the law authorizes it but because the judge is entitled to take *all the circumstances of the parties* into account. One of the circumstances, obviously, is need.

What If Your Supported Ex-Spouse Remarries?

Jim, an ex-boxer who has taken too many punches, receives $200 monthly in court-ordered spousal support. He meets the girl of his dreams and marries her. Jim loses his $200 a month, and his ex-wife can treat the men at the bar to a round.

Most states have domestic relations laws providing that spousal support ends when the person receiving it remarries. And, of course, marital settlement agreements usually provide for this also.

In some states, for example in Arkansas, Connecticut, Missouri, New Hampshire, and New Mexico, the person paying support must go back to court and have the support terminated by the judge. In other states it stops automatically.

Note that if you have made a settlement with your wife that adjusts your property rights, as opposed to "pure" support payments, the remarriage of your wife will not affect the settlement. This also applies if you make a lump settlement of support — by doing so you take your chances that you might have paid less should she remarry.

What If You Are Paying Spousal Support and You Remarry? If you incur a spousal support obligation that involves periodic payments, meet another woman, and want to start a new family, can you stop or lower your support payments because of your new obligations?

The answer is: generally no. Most courts hold that your former obligations were first in time and importance and that you cannot avoid them by incurring others. However, some judges will lower your support payments, depending on the circumstances.

Changing the Amount of Support

If you included spousal support in a marital settlement agreement, generally the amount and duration of the support cannot be changed unless by further agreement (in the absence of fraud, misrepresentation, and the like).

If a judge has made the support order, you can always go back to him or her (or the court) at a later date and request that the amount or duration of the support be lowered or raised because of *changed circumstances:*

Arthur has had a bad year. He lost his job, was denied unemployment, and broke his leg; his girlfriend also walked out on him. His former wife still demanded that Arthur meet a $200 a month support obligation. Arthur hobbled into court, represented himself, and got the support order changed to $50 a month.

The procedure is very similar to that involved in requesting a change of custody or visitation rights. You may or may not need an attorney, depending on the complexities of the circumstances and the amount of money involved. If you are paying, say, under $300 a month in spousal support and want to lower it, you'll probably be able to represent yourself in court adequately.

Either party — the one paying spousal support or the one

receiving it — may apply to the same court that made the order for a change in the support order. This application may be made at any time before the order terminates.

The person seeking the change must show that there has been a substantial change in the circumstances of one or both of the parties since the order was made. This change in circumstances may affect the *amount* of support or the *duration* of support payments.

The kind of circumstances referred to includes a change in the financial circumstances of the party paying support, such as a material change in his or her earnings, earning capacity, assets, or obligations.

Martin, an Ohio dentist, was ordered to pay $1,250 per month spousal support for seven years. A year after the final decree of divorce, he incurred physical ailments and had to reduce his working hours and limit his practice. The spousal support was ordered to be decreased to $750 per month.

Tom had been an unlucky horseplayer for years. His luck was so bad that his wife divorced him. On the chance that someday he might cash a winning ticket, his wife asked for and got a court order awarding her token alimony. When Tom finally did become a winner, so did his ex-wife. Her support order was modified upward to reflect Tom's better fortune.

The reduced expectations of the person paying support may justify a change.

In an Iowa case, the husband's support payments were based on his reasonable expectation of a promotion and an increase in salary. Both fell through, and his later request for a lowering of support was granted.

A spouse cannot ask for a lowering of support payments when his or her income is reduced deliberately; that is, by his or her own voluntary act. Nor will support be lowered or raised when the final decree or judgment made an allowance for some change in the circumstances.

Vicky grew tired of the routine of her dull job and boring life. She quit her job and decided to take up scuba-diving. When she stopped sending her ex-husband his support payments, he hauled her into court. The judge ordered Vicky to pay, even though she claimed she was broke and unemployed.

When people paying support retire and receive only a pension, they may request that their support payments be modified. And the same is true when they receive reduced income due to poor health.

A change in the financial circumstances of the person receiving support may also justify a change.

Mary received $400 per month support under the original order. One year later she was promoted and her income doubled. Her husband may reasonably request that the support be reduced, provided there are no other changes in Mary's circumstances.

If there has been a substantial unforseen increase in the cost of living (not provided for in an agreement or court order) or if the person paying support is saddled with such increased taxes, he or she may be able to justify a change in support.

In some states, if the person receiving support is engaged in acts of gross misconduct (usually sexual), the spouse paying support may request a reduction (or termination) of support. This is tricky, though, and you'll need a lawyer to sustain this type of request.

Note: Spousal support may not be modified with respect to payments that are already due and owing. These must be caught up before any request for a change will even be listened to.

Enforcement of Spousal Support

Most states these days make a big effort to enforce spousal support orders, especially when the person entitled to them applies for public aid. For willful failure to pay support, a person can be held in contempt of court and, if necessary, jailed. Furthermore, his or her property can be seized to satisfy the support payments (although there are some exceptions).

In many states a judge will order that the person who is to pay spousal support put up some kind of security for payment — either a bond or some other collateral. A judge may not, however, impound that person's personal property.

10
Property: His, Hers, and Theirs

Dividing up marital property is one of the more unpleasant tasks in divorce cases. At a time when both husband and wife are emotionally upset, they must disregard their feelings for the time being and concentrate on dry, legalistic issues that will determine their immediate financial future. But long after many of the emotions have dissipated, the effects of the property division will still be felt by each partner.

If a couple cannot agree on how their property is to be divided, the judge hearing the divorce will divide it according to the law of their particular state. This division will be made either in the interlocutory or final decree or judgment of divorce.

Before the judge can distribute the property, it must be determined who owns it — the husband, the wife, or both. Then it must be decided whether the marital property is to be distributed equally or unequally under the law of that state.

Use of Tax Returns

In our discussion of marital settlement agreements, we referred to the use of income tax returns to verify income, debts, and the like. Most judges will accept tax returns as some evidence of the information contained in them, but you should be somewhat cautious about introducing them.

The financial information in tax returns is subject to various different interpretations that may or may not benefit you.

Need for an Appraiser

Hopefully you will not require a formal appraisal of your marital property, since court-ordered appraisals are expensive and time-consuming. Still, if you and your wife simply cannot agree on the nature and extent of your marital property, an appraiser may be required. If so, try to select one who has worked in divorce matters and understands separate and joint property. (Many items of property cannot be divided, and an experienced appraiser can compensate by re-appraising other items to reach a fair division.)

Who Owns the Property?

The ownership or *status* of the property in question during a divorce case can cause headaches for the judge as well as for you and your wife. For example:

Ben brings $20,000 to his marriage and starts a business in which his new wife is employed. They prosper and invest some of the profits in stock, which also increases in value. Ben's wife becomes pregnant and stays home to care for the child but still helps Ben in the business while at home. They sell the stock and buy a home with part of the net profit.

Suppose Ben and his wife, at this point, decide to get a divorce? Regardless of the law of the state they live in, everyone involved is going to have trouble untangling who owns what and how much. This is one of the reasons that every divorcing couple should do their best to agree on property division before they get to court.

Separate Property Your separate property is any property you owned before you were married or you acquired after marriage by gift, will, or inheritance. Separate property also includes any property you bought from money that was separate property:

Jim has $10,000, which he kept in a separate bank account before and after his marriage. After marriage, he buys stock with it, makes more money, and then buys real estate with the proceeds. The real estate is his separate property.

In *community property* states, the earnings of each spouse are community property, whereas in states that have *property by the entirety* regulations, the earnings of each person are his or her separate property.

Joint Marital Property Joint marital property is property acquired by the husband and wife after they were married in which they both have some interest. Their interest depends on whether they live in a community property state or a "property by the entirety" state. Do not confuse joint *marital* interest with *joint tenancy*, for example. Joint marital interest arises from the marriage itself, joint tenancy from how title is taken.

Title: How the Property Is Held The ownership of property may be determined by title. If the title is in your name, you are presumed to be the sole owner. If the title is held by you and your wife as joint tenants, then you are presumed to own it jointly. Security of title is, of course, important to everyone.

It sounds simple. But consider the following:

Phil lives in Texas and plans to marry Helen in Michigan, where she lives. He sends her money to buy a car to be owned by them as husband and wife. They marry, later they divorce, and Phil discovers the car is registered only in Helen's name as the sole owner.

Phil may be able to show, in court, that Helen violated their agreement and that he has an interest in the car. (If Helen had sold the car, Phil wouldn't have been able to go against the buyer because the title was good on its face.) The same principle is true if real property has been purchased by one person in his or her name only but the other person has a legal interest in it.

Other Forms of Tenancy If the title was taken in *joint tenancy*, both the husband and wife share equally in the ownership, each has the right to use the property, and if one spouse dies, the survivor takes the entire title automatically. However, if the title was registered by husband and wife as *tenants in common*, both spouses own equal shares and may use the property, but if one spouse dies the survivor does *not* take the share of the deceased person unless that has been specified in his or her will. Otherwise, the property passes (to the extent of the interest of the deceased) to that person's nearest blood relative under the laws of the state where the property is located.

Tenancies by the entirety (often referred to as "common law tenancies") are much like joint tenancies, except that they are limited to two persons (joint tenancies are unlimited) and that unless the law permits, tenants by the entirety cannot have their property split up and divided. A divorce, however, converts a common law tenancy into a tenancy in common.

Gift from One Spouse to the Other   Have you ever been Santa Claus and not even known it? It's not hard, particularly in marriage transactions that we all more or less take for granted. For example:

Bob owns an expensive home and plans to marry Trudy. After they marry, Bob changes title from himself as sole owner to joint tenancy with Trudy. Later they divorce, and Bob proves the house was originally his and that Trudy contributed nothing to its purchase or maintenance.

Bob is probably out of luck. Legally, he has made a gift to Trudy of half of the house, unless he can produce solid evidence (more than his own testimony) that he intended no such thing.

The same principle applies to transfers or purchases of personal property:

George owned a car before he married Barbara. After the marriage, he registered the car to himself and Barbara. George has made a gift of one-half interest in the car to Barbara.

The same is true when you pay for property purchased by your wife. For example:

Betty buys a fur coat without telling her husband, Art. Art gets the bill and pays it out of his separate savings or stock account.

Art has made a gift of at least half of the coat (and perhaps all of it) to his wife.

How about such transfers from your wife to you — does it work both ways? In some states yes, in others no. But even in those states where the answer is yes, it is much harder for an attorney to prove something was a gift from a wife to a husband than vice versa. There is a *de facto* presumption that the husband is more likely to exploit the wife than the other way around. Consequently, more protection is afforded the wife.

Note: If you find yourself in a situation like this and the judge decides that you made a gift to your wife, remember that giving and receiving gifts have tax consequences.

Community Property: Property by the Entirety Under early common law, a married woman lost her separate property and was largely unprotected when she married. Certain laws, called the Married Women's Acts, were passed in order to protect the property that a woman owned when she married and keep it as her own separate property.

As to property acquired *after* marriage, two general systems have developed — community property and property by the entirety. Both systems do the same thing in effect; namely, they give both married people an interest in property they acquire by their effort or earnings.

Community property is all the property acquired by either spouse during marriage *except* that acquired by a gift, by a will, or by inheritance.

Sid and Alison marry. Both work, and they open a joint bank account, buy a house, and invest in the stock market. Sid's father gives him a boat, and Alison's mother leaves her some property, which she sells. She reinvests the proceeds in gold futures. The only community property they own is the joint bank account, the house, and the stocks. The rest is separate property.

Property by the entirety (called the "common law rule") is much like community property; that is, husband and wife hold the property as equals until they die or until the marriage is dissolved. Property by the entirety is also much like property held in joint tenancy, except that there may be any number of joint tenants in property, whereas under the common law rule there may only be two.

Pete and Alice Johnson live in Indiana. Pete's mother deeds some real estate to "Pete and Alice Johnson." She also endorses some stock certificates over to them in the same manner. Pete and Alice jointly own the real estate and stocks as tenants in the entirety.

Equal or Unequal Distribution?

Separate Property   Upon divorce, each spouse is given his or her separate property, regardless of which state they live in. The court has no power to transfer any of your separate property (or that of your wife) to anyone, including your spouse. Your own, separate property *is* liable for your debts, however.

Community Property States   In states using the community property system, the distribution of marital property upon divorce varies.

Community property states are:

Arizona	Louisiana	Puerto Rico
California	Nevada	Texas
Idaho	New Mexico	Washington

Fault (marital misconduct) may increase or decrease a married person's otherwise equal share of community property in the above states except for Arizona, California, and Washington (where fault has been eliminated as a ground for divorce). And in all of the above states except for Arizona, California, and Washington, the court may, in fairness, distribute community property unequally, according to the circumstances. In the three states excepted, the court *must* distribute the community property equally.

Common Law States (by Entirety)   In several states still operating under the common law property system, when married persons divorce the court has no power to distribute property; matters are decided according to the title to the property (subject to exceptions of fraud and the like). These states are:

Florida   Pennsylvania   Virginia
Mississippi   Tennessee   West Virginia
New York

However, thirty-seven states that still recognize the common law property system permit a judge to distribute joint property unequally, to achieve fairness under the circumstances. These states are:

Alabama (as to   Kansas   North Dakota
  alimony only)   Kentucky   Ohio (as to
Alaska   Maine   alimony only)
Arkansas   Maryland   Oklahoma
Colorado   Massachusetts   Oregon
Connecticut   Michigan   Rhode Island
Delaware   Minnesota   South Carolina
District of   Missouri   South Dakota
  Columbia   Montana   Tennessee
Georgia (as to   Nebraska   Utah
  alimony only)   New Hampshire   Vermont
Hawaii   New Jersey   Wisconsin
Illinois   North Carolina   Wyoming
Indiana   (as to alimony
Iowa   only)

Note: Some states (such as Maryland) may make a money award to one spouse in lieu of property distribution. Note also that some states require that premarital property be distributed as well as marital property; that is, where the parties have made a premarital agreement, the property included will be subject to the same rules as the marital property.

Criteria Used for Unequal Distribution   In those states where a judge may distribute marital property unequally, what are the considerations used to make the distribution? The most frequently used are:

• the contributions of each spouse to the marriage
• the marital assets generally
• the financial condition of the spouse seeking support and the spouse from whom it is sought

- the present and prospective earnings of each spouse
- the skills and needs of the custodial parent and the desirability of the custodial parent remaining at home to care for the children
- how long the marriage lasted
- the age, health, and financial circumstances of each spouse
- the amount and sources of income of each
- the standard of living enjoyed by each during the marriage

The Home: Occupancy, Sale, and Distribution

Assuming your home is community property or some other form of joint marital property in which both you and your wife have a substantial interest, disposing of it is frequently among the biggest headaches facing a divorcing man.

A family home is an appreciating asset but needs upkeep. It produces no income until it is sold (or rented), and if the mortgage or trust deed payments are heavy, it may be a financial drain. If you or your wife are offered the home in exchange for other community assets, it would be wise to think carefully before assuming sole ownership.

In many instances, of course, circumstances dictate that your wife take the home as her share of the marital property. In that case, you would probably want her to take over payment of the mortgage, taxes, insurance, maintenance, and so on. The catch is that the bank or savings and loan company holding the mortgage probably will not let you off the paper. If this is the case and the home is not to be sold, the best you can do is have your wife guarantee the payment of these expenses and, in the process, indemnify you from any losses from her failure to pay. She may well demand, as the price of such a guarantee, that it be contingent on you making your monthly support payments (if you owe them).

Wife as Occupant: Joint Ownership   One solution to disposing of the family home is an arrangement whereby you both continue to hold title as joint tenants or tenants in common, with your ex-wife having possession of the property for a given period of time (perhaps until the children are a given age or your ex-wife remarries). If this appears feasible, you must also agree on the disposition of the sale proceeds. This is because the equity in the house will appreciate because of both the loan reduction and inflation.

If your ex-wife makes the loan payments, she has a good claim to the increased equity but not necessarily to any appreciation in the house's market value. You can legitimately argue that you are losing interest on your investment, your ex-wife is using the house rent-free, and that the money she is using for the payments is your support money (if this is the case).

Obviously, these problems are best worked out in a marital settlement agreement. In many instances, the quickest and easiest solution is simply to agree that the net proceeds will be divided equally when the house is sold.

Enforcement of Agreement to Sell

Jerry and Sonja are divorcing and agree to sell their house and divide the proceeds. Just before escrow opens, Sonja backs out and refuses to go ahead with the sale. Will the court force her to sign the necessary papers?

Generally, yes. When divorcing parties agree to sell their property and divide the money, the court will usually enforce the agreement rather than listen to a lawsuit for damages for breach of contract.

Occupancy of Home Pending Sale The courts are very unpredictable on the question of occupancy of the family home. For example, in New York:

Where there are no children and the wife shows no need to reside in the family home, it should be sold and the proceeds divided equally.
[Sharer vs. Sharer, 400 NYS2d 423, 1977]

The trial court acted properly in awarding the wife exclusive possession of the home.
[Biven vs. Biven, 404 NYS2d 185, 1978]

If your wife has been awarded custody of the children, the judge will probably allow her to use the family home until it is sold or until her financial circumstances permit her to move. The same will be true for you, should you receive custody of the children.

If no children are involved, you can toss a coin — as the above cases indicate. In any event, the spouse occupying the home temporarily should pay a reasonable rent to the other, provided the circumstances justify it.

John and Carol divorce. Under the terms of the final decree, John is given the family home. He permits Carol to stay there until she finds a suitable place. After three months, John realizes she doesn't intend to move and tries to evict her.

John is within his rights. Carol uses the property as a "licensee" (legalese for "at John's sufferance"), and her "license" expires when John tells her to move. *Note:* A landlord is not bound by an agreement between divorcing spouses that one agrees to let the other keep the rented premises.

The Home as Security for a Loan Suppose you need security for a loan that is to go to your wife as all or part of an overall settlement? You should ask your wife to transfer her interest in the property to you and use the property as security for the loan. In another situation, it might work well for you to transfer your interest in the property to your wife so that she can sell it, buy another house, and receive beneficial capital gains tax treatment (sale of principal residence and purchase of another).

Alternatively, your wife might want to buy you out of the house and finance the purchase of your interest herself. You may, of course, demand any terms for the sale that suit you, taking into consideration your tax picture, but our advice would be to stay flexible. Go ahead and take a second mortgage or trust deed to secure the loan, if that will work for you.

Sale: Distribution of Proceeds If the family home is to be sold, you and your wife must agree on the terms of sale.

Otherwise the judge will order it to be sold at its fair market value. So-called "forced" sales like these are attractive to potential buyers who feel they can obtain the property for less than its real value.

Both you and your wife should consult a real estate person who is acceptable to you both and who should be instructed that at closing of escrow, the net proceeds from the sale are to be distributed according to either the agreement you have made or the court order for distribution. If either you or your ex-wife have maintained the property while it was vacant, those expenses should be credited to the proper person.

If you have been forced to take a second mortgage or trust deed on the sale, you are both free to offer the other a cash price for that person's interest in the second. It may be of benefit to one or both of you, depending on your tax situation.

If one of you is to occupy the home for a substantial period of time before the sale, the equity of each of you should be agreed upon before the occupancy begins. After that, the considerations of mortgage payments, cost of upkeep, taxes, and so on become largely a matter for your accountant.

Personal Property

Personal property includes all property that is not real estate (except the house and buildings on the real estate). As is true with real estate, personal property can be the separate property of either spouse or the joint property of both. For example:

When Jeff was married, he owned an automobile, electronic equipment, some stocks, and had $2,000 in the bank. Roseanne, his wife, had her car, some furniture, and $5,000 in the bank. Each kept this property separate. During marriage they bought, from their earnings, a boat, a trailer, and some art objects. Only the items they bought after marriage are jointly owned by them.

The following are some of the types of personal property in which both husband and wife usually have some interest:
- life insurance
- employee benefits

- stocks, bonds, and notes
- business interests
- automobiles
- household furniture and furnishings
- personal effects
- interests in trusts
- bank accounts
- credit union accounts

Earnings after Separation but before Divorce Final In most states, from the time husband and wife separate the wife's earnings (as well as those of the children if she has them) are her own. By contrast, in many states the husband's earnings during this same period are *not* his separate property until either an interlocutory decree of divorce is issued or a final decree. This seems unfair and should be changed.

Personal Effects: Household Furnishings Probably nothing is so likely to produce ill will, bickering, and aggravation as two divorcing people trying to divide up silver, television sets, furniture, and the like. You'd be well advised to keep your temper, as well as your sense of humor, when taking on this chore. Of course, ideally you and your wife should have divided up your household and personal effects before you tried to make an agreement or go to court. If you haven't, read on.

In general, household goods acquired by husband and wife for their mutual use and enjoyment are joint property. *Warning:* If you cannot agree on ownership of the household goods, some courts will order them sold and the proceeds divided. Not only does such a sale cost money, but since it is a "forced" sale, you can expect that the property will not bring what it is worth.

When Ed and Margaret were married, they found, among their gifts, an expensive silver set from Margaret's mother. The gift was inscribed to "the newlyweds."

Who owns the silver? The law is that wedding gifts are presumed to be joint marital property. Ed and Margaret will have to sell the set and split the proceeds or work out some other equitable arrangement.

In the event that you have carried insurance on personal property in the home (usually homeowner's insurance) and the property is transferred to your wife, you should transfer the policy to her name and give it to her when the divorce decree is final. (And vice versa, of course.) And any documents of title should be given to the spouse taking the property so that he or she can prove ownership if the need arises later. A good example of this is signing over the document of title in your automobile, if that is appropriate.

Retirement and Pension Benefits   The trend is to award a community interest in retirement and pension benefits, provided such benefits are vested. Some states holding this view are community property states and others are common law states. These states include:

California	Louisiana	New Mexico
Colorado	Michigan	Texas
Florida	Nebraska	Washington
Idaho	New Jersey	Wisconsin

Liability Insurance: Conversion and Renewal   Several states have laws providing that accident and health insurance policies that automatically terminate on divorce must also contain a conversion privilege by the divorced spouse (the beneficiary), even though he or she does not offer proof of insurability. Examples of these states are Illinois, South Carolina, and Wisconsin. Check on this law in your state, since the trend is toward such conversion privileges.

It is not uncommon that a woman who is divorced must pay a higher premium for automobile liability insurance than while she was married. If you wish, permit your wife to continue on the joint policy until the marriage is ended by a final decree. You are taking some risk in doing this, of course, but if it turns out badly you can always cancel at short-term rates.

Life Insurance: Problems and Solutions   For many

married people, life insurance policies are among their most valuable assets. Cash surrender values have often been built up over the years and represent the community savings. Moreover, even in term insurance, where there is little or no cash surrender value, policies are useful in reaching practical solutions to property distribution.

The amount of interest that you and your wife have in life insurance policies is determined by the source of the funds used to purchase the policies. If the premiums were paid from community or marital funds (such as wages), then the policies are marital property to that extent.

Suppose you and your wife have a life insurance policy with a valuable cash surrender value. What are some of the ways you can deal with this property without necessarily terminating it? In addition to surrendering the policy and dividing the proceeds, you can:

- Assign your rights in the policy to the other spouse for a price or other consideration, or vice versa.
- Partition the existing policy (a legal procedure where your respective interests are split up but the policy is not surrendered).
- Convert the existing policy to another type of coverage or, where possible, to an annuity contract.
- Assign the policy to the other spouse, one spouse to pay the premiums (again, for other consideration).
- Designate your children as beneficiaries.
- Purchase new coverage.

Note: You may need to surrender the policy and distribute the proceeds because of marital debts. But you should consider other means of raising the money, since the cost and availability of new insurance may be open to question if you are an older man with any health problems.

Ideally, a husband should seek award of the policy without any requirement that he designate a beneficiary. Most men will marry again and will want their new wife to have insurance protection. If you are required to maintain the children as beneficiaries on the policy, your attorney should seek to limit the time period (until they are of age, married, or emancipated).

Debts Any secured creditor, of course, can reach the asset securing a marital obligation, whether you are divorced or not. And if you (or your wife) are on a note or credit obligation, the fact that you are getting divorced won't change matters (except to make your creditor nervous). Also, if you and your wife together have incurred a debt, you are both liable — individually and jointly — and the marital property may be subject to enforcement of the debt if it comes to that.

Debts are listed together with assets when the judge makes the property distribution. The sensible thing, of course, is for you and your wife to agree on payment of the debts to suit your individual finances and conveniences. For example, you may want the family automobile, on which $500 is still owing. Your wife may sign the car over to you for an amount that represents her equity (discounted), provided you take over the remainder of the payments.

You and your wife probably have unsecured debts, such as credit card obligations and installment accounts of one kind or another. Without getting overly complicated, regardless of whose name the account is in, if the benefits of the debt were received by the marital community, then the marital community (rather than separate property) should be used to satisfy the debt. Gasoline credit cards used for the family car are a good example, even though they may be in the husband's name only.

Suppose you make a marital settlement agreement under which you will owe your wife money? This is common, for example, when a marital asset is the husband's business, which he wants to continue operating but his wife does not. Once your wife's interest (if any) in the business can be determined, you have some choices, provided you can't come up with the money immediately:

- Give her a promissory note for the amount.
- Give her a note secured by the assets of the business.
- Consider a trade-off for some other marital property of similar value.
- Borrow the money from another source and, if necessary, pledge the business and assets.
- Issue non-voting stock to her in the business, if possible and appropriate.

If you will owe your ex-wife money after the divorce, try to satisfy the debt as soon as possible. Otherwise, you'll wind up in many of the problems that you tried to leave behind when you obtained your divorce.

Division: Some Possibilities   As regards the distribution of your personal property, here are some of the possibilities you and your wife can consider:
- straight division with absolute ownership in one spouse
- agreement to divide up the property within a specified time or submit to arbitration
- one party to receive all or part of the property in return for assumption of obligations
- one party to receive all household goods after a certain date, the other party to use in the meantime
- one party to purchase the other's interest in all or any items
- property to be sold in entirety and proceeds split according to agreement
- property to be appraised and amount of appraisal credited to party not receiving property
- party agreeing to pay support credited for amount of his or her interest — other person keeping property

Making a New Will

Mark and Gwen are divorced in 1979, after seven years of marriage and two children. He is killed in an automobile accident in 1980 and among his personal effects is found a will dated 1978 leaving everything he has to Gwen, his former wife. Mark's children and parents contest the will.

Whether Mark's children and his parents can upset the will depends on what state the will is probated in. The situation involves what lawyers call "implied revocation." This legal fiction means that had the person making the will thought of it, he or she probably would have revoked the will after the divorce. In other words, the circumstances after the divorce probably changed the *intent* of the testator (the person making the will).

Some states, such as Michigan, have specific laws under which Mark's heirs and children would be successful in their suit. However, California, Ohio, and New York reject this legal rule. You can avoid this problem altogether, of course, if you remember to make a new will after you divorce.

If you are reluctant to make a new will because you feel you may reconcile with your wife and don't want to embarrass everyone, make the will anyway but provide that it is to be effective only upon a final decree.

PART III

DIVORCE AND SEPARATION: THE CHILD

11
Rules for Determining Custody

Because the love, solicitude, and devotion of a mother cannot
be replaced by another and are worth more to a child of tender years
than all other things combined, a child should not be deprived of the
necessary and wholesome influences of these characteristics of a mother
if it can be reasonably avoided.
[Bath vs. Bath, 150 Nebraska 591, 1949]

The natural inclination to give to the mother the custody of her children
of tender years is a recognition that the mother is God's own institution
for the rearing and upbringing of children, and given to the mother
in preference to the father, even though the latter may have been without
fault and may have been awarded the divorce.
[Hines vs. Hines, 192 Iowa 569, 1921]

Maternal Preference Rule

Until the end of the last century, fathers were entitled to the custody of their children. This rule then gave way to the more flexible practice that the best interests of the child should prevail in custody proceedings.

The best interests rule was honored more in the breach than in the observance, however. Judges paid lip service to the idea, while holding in most cases that "a mother's love is so important to a child that the child should be given to the mother in preference to the father." [*Bath vs. Bath 150 Nebr 591, 1949*].

Some reasons given for this preference were that the mother is the natural custodian of the young, and that her love for her child is irreplaceable:

The presumption favoring the mother over the father in awarding custody of their children springs from the truth, well known by all men, that no other love is quite so tender, no other solicitude quite so deep, and no other devotion quite so enduring as that of a mother for her child.
[Horst vs. McLain, Missouri, 466 SW2d 187, 1971]

The recent award-winning film, *Kramer vs. Kramer,* dramatically presented the unfairness and heartache that often result from the maternal preference rule.

The Presumption — What Does It Mean?   Under the maternal preference rule, the mother rather than the father is *presumed* to be the proper custodial parent. Furthermore, she is presumed to be a fit mother.

A presumption, in law, means that the truth of what is asserted need not be proven; that is, the plaintiff (the mother) need not give any evidence on the subject or, for that matter, even testify as to her fitness. Rather, the respondent (the father) is required to prove that the mother is *not* fit to be the custodial parent, and when he tries to do this, he is met by another presumption — that the mother *is* fit. Does this sound irrational? It is — but then legalese has rarely been accused of being rational.

As a result of maternal preference, desperate fathers are sometimes driven to use desperate and ugly means to protect their children. Often, proving maternal unfitness demands that a father must stoop to "getting the goods" on his ex-wife, making public episodes that were better forgotten, spying, exaggerating, attempting to destroy the child's relationship with the mother, and lying in court.

And matching the desperate father is the desperate mother. Most women will go to almost any lengths to avoid being labeled an "unfit mother." The advances of the women's movement and the end of mandatory motherhood have not removed the sting from this label. A mother may accept, with difficulty, that it is better for her child to be with his or her father. But she can almost never tolerate being labeled "unfit."

The Lingering Influence of the Rule   Only two states (Oklahoma and South Dakota) still have the maternal preference rule on their books. Many states abandoned the rule out of common sense; others because they equalized their laws governing domestic relations. However, to date the best interests rule has been enacted into law in less than thirty-five states.

If only two states still have laws that give the mother preference in custody battles, you might ask, What's the problem? The answer is that the law as written and the law as made by judges ("case law") are not necessarily the same. As far as the maternal preference rule is concerned, this is patently true.

In many states the maternal preference rule is no longer part of the law, but cases are nonetheless decided as though it *were* still part of the law — probably because of the continuing reluctance of judges to take a child from his or her mother. Understandably perhaps, many judges still feel that awarding the custody of a child to the father stigmatizes the mother. Finally, it's a good guess that more mothers are ready to do battle for their children than are fathers.

Thus the former status quo is perpetuated. By and large, mothers are still awarded custody of their children — particularly children of "tender years" (under five or ten years old).

Luckily, the days of the maternal presumption are numbered — as they should be. A child is not a piece of property that either parent has a right to have. Nor should a child be lumped with the bank balance and other personal effects to be divided up in the aftermath of a fractured relationship.

A child is a person — and the person most directly affected by custody decisions. His or her needs as a growing individual must come before the parents' rights vis-à-vis each other. And they must come before legal convenience and tradition.

Fighting for Custody in a Maternal Preference State
Custody fights are almost always unpleasant. However, when the mother's fitness becomes the issue, court proceed-

181

ings are particularly destructive. Mothers must be maligned; parents never overcome their bitterness; lawyers get ulcers and rich; children lose respect for their parents, parents lose their self-respect; and all parties lose respect for the law.

We believe that the more often men justly fight for custody of their children, the sooner the maternal presumption will be abolished. You, however, as a father, are probably more concerned with the welfare of your child than the need for changing the law. You who will have to decide whether the advantage of the possibility of your having custody outweighs the damage that fighting for custody will bring.

Some of the drawbacks of unfitness proceedings include the following:

- It is almost impossible to shield your child from the bitterness involved.
- Children need to have a mother and a father they can respect. Both of you will be devalued in court.
- Children inevitably feel forced to side with one parent or the other.
- A cooperative relationship between you and your child's mother is beneficial to your child, no matter who has custody. This will be almost impossible after an unfitness fight.
- The monetary cost is high.

The "Best Interests" Rule

In most states, custody and visitation are determined by what is in the *best interests* of the child, and there is no preference as to which parent is the more suitable custodian — at least not on the books. Most of these states have "de-sexed" their laws, and many have laws similar to the proposed national Equal Rights Amendment.

The best interests standard puts first the needs and rights of the person most affected by a custody decision — the child. Obviously, a child is not a person alone. He or she is part of a family, and the rights and needs of the parents must be recognized too. Using the child's best interests as the basis for a custody decision allows the rights of the parents to be respected, gives the child the opportunity of two possible custody situations, but still places the priority where it belongs — with the child.

Proving Best Interests   In states where the best interests rule is the law, an assessment is made of the child's emotional, physical, and educational needs, and both parents try to show how their having custody would benefit the child. The judge considers all the facts and tries to make the best decision possible for the child.

Paula feels that she must leave her hard-drinking husband, Al. She is convinced that their daughter, Shirley, must be in her custody. Al will set a bad example, she tells her lawyer, and he probably won't live much longer anyway, the way he's going. Al counters that in spite of his drinking he has supported his family, provided daily care for Shirley, attended PTA meetings, and repaired the house throughout their eight-year marriage.

In a maternal presumption state, Paula would have the undisputed right to rear little Shirley. But in "best interest states," the situation is much more complicated. All the following points are relevant to deciding custody: What is the quality of Shirley's relationship with each of her parents? Who has provided most of Shirley's daily care? What is the status of each of the parents' health? Will Al's habits affect Shirley's health? Is the bad example Al sets by drinking offset by his teaching Sunday School?

This, of course, is an extremely subjective and imprecise way to make a decision. To some extent, every facet of the character and life of the child and each parent is relevant in deciding what is in the best interests of the child. The judge naturally has biases in these matters. He or she must take these personal biases, balance the advantages and disadvantages of both parents, and come to a reasonable decision.

To eliminate some of the subjectivity, state laws generally require that certain factors must be considered in determining best interests. Among these are usually the following:
- the character and financial resources of each parent
- the temperamental fitness of each parent to care for the child

- the environment in each parent's home or prospective home
- the parents' actions and attitudes toward the child in the past
- the age and health of each parent
- the prospective advantages that may be given to the child in the event that custody is awarded to either parent
- the age, sex, physical and emotional condition of the child
- the wishes or preference of the child (depending, of course, on the child's age and intelligence)
- each parent's religious beliefs or lack of them insofar as either might adversely affect the child
- the history, if any, of drunkenness, drug addiction, or criminal acts by either parent
- the testimony of each parent at the custody hearing and how the judge weighs it

Obviously, the above list is not exhaustive. Each judge has particular items he or she may consider that other judges may not consider. And each judge is a human being who puts different stress on different items. The best interests rule means just that — judges may, at their discretion, rule as *they* see fit.

Third Person Custody   Neither you nor your wife has an absolute right to the custody of your child under the best interests test, although the parental preference rule (adopted in virtually all states) gives the parents preference over non-parents.

Nevertheless, when the best interests of the child are not served by parental custody, the judge may award custody to a third person such as a grandparent or foster parent.

"Fault" — Is It Important?   In most states, the "fault" of one parent or the other (as "fault" is used in divorce cases) is not considered *directly* in determining custody. Still, judges in some states consider the moral character of the parents (in Utah, for example), the lifestyle of the parents (in Oregon), or the fault of the parents (in South Dakota) as each may be relevant to the *fitness* of a parent as custodian. In other words, fault in fact *is* considered frequently, although perhaps by other names.

Appointing an Attorney for the Child

Some states, recognizing that the child is the most important party to custody proceedings, have passed laws providing for the appointment of a guardian *ad litem* (temporary guardian only for the court case) to represent the child's interests in custody battles. These states also usually provide for investigations and reports to the judges, as well as for interviewing the child privately in the judge's chambers.

Wisconsin, for example, has a law providing that in all domestic relations cases where custody of a child is at issue, the judge *must* appoint such a guardian to represent the child. Check in your state to see if you have such a law — it could assist you in a custody fight and save you some money.

States with Equal Custody Rights Laws

Below is a list of the states where the domestic relations law has been de-sexed with regard to child custody or where the law equalizes parental rights to child custody:

Alaska	Idaho	New Jersey
Arkansas	Indiana	New York
California	Kansas	North Carolina
Colorado	Kentucky	North Dakota
Connecticut	Louisiana	Ohio
Delaware	Massachusetts	Oregon
District of	Minnesota	Tennessee
Columbia	Montana	Texas
Florida	Nebraska	Virginia
Georgia	Nevada	Wisconsin
Hawaii	New Hampshire	Wyoming

Some states have specific laws that authorize the joint custody of children; for example, California, Iowa, Oregon, North Carolina, and Wisconsin. Joint custody is discussed in Chapter Thirteen.

12
When and How to Obtain Custody

*Before long there will be some order which will have some degree
of permanency to the end that the child will be reared in, and have
the benefits of, a home grounded upon decency, respectability, stability,
sound character, and love.*
                    [Saltonstall vs. Saltonstall, 1952, 148 CA2d 109]

In the latter half of the seventies, more and more judges in
more and more courts were required to decide child custody
disputes. There is every indication that this trend will accel-
erate during the eighties.

One reason for this is, of course, the rapidly rising divorce
rate. A more important reason, however, is that most states
have equalized their domestic relations laws and with a few
exceptions, fathers now stand on a more equal footing with
their wives or partners in matters of child custody. And
lawyers, once reluctant to represent fathers in child custody
battles and then only at an exhorbitant fee, are more willing
to fight for fathers' rights.

Still the *de facto* influence of the maternal preference rule
discourages many fathers from seeking custody of their children. This bias in our legal system, though diminishing,
often frustrates fathers even when there is abundant evidence
pointing to their suitability as custodian. Conversely,
mothers are encouraged to seek and accept custody even
though it may not be in their or their children's best interests.
It is interesting to note that, of those fathers who fight for
their children, almost half are successful. By 1978 there were

more than one million children being successfully raised by recently divorced fathers.

By and large, the evidence shows that single fathers parent their children as well as do single mothers, and in some instances better. For some single fathers, however, custody is more than they bargained for. The day-to-day responsibilities of a custodial parent often prove onerous to single fathers — particularly those whose involvement with their children was minimal before the divorce. The moral? Be careful of what you wish for. You may get it!

Fathers seeking custody of their children today are offered a number of choices not available in the past. Depending on the circumstances, they may obtain sole custody, split or divided custody, or even joint custody of their children.

What Does Custody Mean?

In divorce proceedings, child custody may be thought of as *child guardianship*. Child custodians, like guardians, have the legal duty to take care of the child and his or her property. The legal custody of a child ends when the child is of age or is emancipated; that is, living independently of the custodial parent. If the custodial parent dies or becomes unable to function properly, the non-custodial parent is usually appointed as the custodial parent unless this arrangement would not be in the child's best interests.

Note: If you remarry, this does not, of itself, change your responsibility as a custodial parent. Your new partner may assume some of the legal responsibility for the child if she legally adopts him or her. But you are still primarily liable for the child's welfare even though this duty is now shared.

What Authority Does the Custodial Parent Have?

A custodial parent has pretty much the same rights and duties to his or her child after the divorce as before. The chief difference is that these rights and duties are no longer shared. (Joint custody is an exception, of course.)

If you have been awarded custody of your child, you and you alone have the power to exercise parental rights over the child. But, you and you alone are also responsible for the child's acts.

Jim obtains sole custody of his daughter, Rachel, after a bitter court fight. Rachel, upset by the fighting, burns down the school house. Jim is liable (in most states); his former wife is not.

As the custodial parent, you have the authority to make decisions regarding your child's care and control, health, religion, and education. You also have the right to decide where you and the children are to live. This right, however, is subject to the terms of the divorce decree or judgment, which usually prohibits the removal of the children from the jurisdiction of the court without permission.

How Is Custody Decided?

By Agreement Child custody may be and frequently is agreed to by the parents. Custody stipulations are part of the marital settlement agreement in most instances but may be included in living-together agreements as well.

Custody agreements will ordinarily be approved by the judge hearing your divorce case, provided the agreement protects the best interests of the child. Custody agreements usually are accompanied by further agreements covering visitation and child support.

After judges approve custody agreements, they generally incorporate them word-for-word or by reference in their final divorce decrees or judgments. Custody agreements then have the force of court orders and may be enforced as such.

By Court Order In most instances, if the person filing for divorce requests that he or she be granted temporary custody of the children, the judge will grant the order. An order for temporary custody is effective until it is changed into or replaced by a permanent order when the divorce proceedings are over.

Temporary custody orders are extremely important because months and even years may pass between the temporary custody hearing and the main court trial; because judges are very reluctant to remove a child from a home situation where he or she is doing well; and because judges are apt to award temporary possession of the home to the custodial parent so that the child's life will be less disturbed.

The following two cases use language expressing clearly the courts' reluctance to upset the status quo:

We cannot be insensitive to the fact . . . that the stability of the home life of the children is an important and vital factor . . . . In view of this . . . it was to Edward's interest not to have his accustomed mode of living [with his father] and home environment abruptly changed.
[Fine vs. Denny, 1952, 111 CA2d 402]

And:

So this court agrees . . . that this boy should not be moved around anymore. He has been domiciled with his father for some time.
[Norton vs. Norton, 1952, 112 CA2d 358]

In short, once the child and the custodial parent have "settled in," the judge may view the arrangement as satisfactory and order it to be made permanent.

Obviously, if child custody is important to you, it is very advantageous to make the first move. If possible, file for the divorce yourself and request temporary custody of the children. In addition, you should consider requesting the possession of the family home until a hearing is scheduled. (This depends on the circumstances, of course. Few judges will evict a wife from the home unless her behavior is so offensive that the children may be harmed.) In any event, you'll have a chance to make an impressive beginning as a custodial father in surroundings familiar to the kids. By the time your divorce is tried in court, you'll have solid evidence of your fitness as a single custodial father.

Suppose, though, that your wife has filed for divorce and has already obtained temporary custody of the children? Even though you are now in a defensive position, you should gear up for a good fight at the hearing on the temporary custody order (usually about ten days or so after the order is issued).

To make much of a case for changing the order, you'll need to show you have made arrangements that are suitable for child-care, including, where necessary, day-care, schooling, and the like. As always, you must show that the best interests of the children dictate that temporary custody should be awarded to you. Even if you lose at this temporary hearing, remember that the ball game isn't over yet. You'll have another chance at the trial of the divorce. More on this later.

Under some circumstances, it may be best to take the children with you and leave the home before any papers are filed. Women have traditionally done this without hesitation, and so can you — with or without a note on the kitchen sink.

If you feel such a move is demanded in the best interests of the child, *call your lawyer and let him or her know what you plan to do.* Be sure to notify the school authorities and anyone else concerned with the child's welfare. Above all, of course, you must have a suitable place to care for the child until the legalities are straightened out. Probably the easiest arrangement would be for you and your child to stay with a relative.

Permanent Custody Orders During or after the court trial of your divorce, the judge will make a "permanent" custody order. Permanent is in quotes because even a permanent custody order may be changed later under certain circumstances. If the permanent order is against the law, as your lawyer sees it, you have the right to appeal. You may not appeal a temporary custody order.

Don was served with divorce papers and his wife was temporarily given the house and children. Don was ordered to pay temporary spousal and child support. Before the trial, nine months later, Don obtained evidence indicating that the temporary arrangement was no longer in the children's best interests. The judge may, after hearing Don's evidence, change the temporary custody order and award Don custody on the grounds of changed circumstances.

What Effect Do Court Orders Have?

If you and your wife have made an oral agreement concerning custody that is not contained in the judge's final order, neither of you are bound by it. The judge's final order establishes that the custodial parent is a suitable person to have custody. In addition, it cuts off the rights of all other persons to have custody.

When the custodial parent consults with the other parent about the child's welfare, he or she does so without legal obligation. This is a difficult position for men with strong paternal feelings. If you find yourself in this position, swallow your feeling as best you can and concentrate on making your visitation rights meaningful. However, if you are the custodial parent, consult with the mother whenever the best interests of the child dictate. And do it with some consideration.

What Is Your Motivation?

Child custody should never be used to harass or acquire power over your ex-partner. This power, even if it could be gained, could never compensate you for the time, energy, and money that is required of a single parent.

Often one parent will use the threat of a custody fight to obtain leverage in settlement negotiations. Don't do this — and if your wife does, don't cave in.

Tim, a traveling sales rep, has three children under ten. He is seldom in one place for more than a week and cannot change jobs. His wife sues Tim for divorce and requests custody of the children. Tim lies awake nights worrying whether he should fight her request as a matter of principle to show everyone, including his children, that he cares.

Don't fight an otherwise reasonable custody arrangement because you feel you must, that you are morally bound to. You're not — unless the best interests of the children demand that you are. Forget any phony pride you may have; it's not only irrelevant, it can be damaging. You'll have plenty of time after the smoke dies down to show the kids you love them.

The best single fathers are generally those who actively seek custody of their children — who want custody and will fight for it. The worst single fathers are those who receive custody through default, for example, when the woman has left and the man has little choice.

Ask yourself the following questions and answer them as honestly as you can, remembering that the interests of your child are at stake:

- Before I separated, did I spend some time with the kids over and above my role as a father? Did I enjoy it?
- Am I familiar with most of their day-to-day problems and how they deal with them?
- Have I been actively involved in the discipline of the kids?
- Will I have the emotional and financial resources to meet my own needs as well as theirs?
- Have I looked for some help and education about some of the problems I'll face? Do I plan to?
- Am I willing to change my lifestyle, if necessary, to accommodate the needs of the kids?
- Am I willing to make substantial sacrifices of time and money to help nurture the kids?
- Have I *really ended* my relationship with their mother?
- Am I trying to hurt my wife or avoid child support payments?
- *Do I honestly feel that the children would be better off with me than with my wife?*

There are other questions, of course, but these may give you some insight into your motivation for seeking the custody of your children. One thing to remember: your kids will quickly smoke out why you want custody of them — even if you don't level with them and yourself.

Custody Investigations

Most states have a procedure whereby the judge hearing a child custody dispute is assisted by interested persons or agencies who make investigations and recommendations. These persons may be social workers, probation department personnel, court-appointed investigators, and so on. Whoever they are in your state, their function is pretty much the same everywhere.

Costs   In some states, the costs of a custody investigation are borne by the court (or county). In other states, one or both parents may be required to pay for or share the costs, depending on their financial circumstances.

How Are Investigations Ordered?   The domestic relations department in most state courts automatically refers contested child custody cases to the investigative agency. If such a referral is not made or if you're in doubt as to whether this procedure is available, your attorney should advise you.

You (through your attorney) should request such an investigation when it is in the best interests of your child; for example, if you feel it would be harmful or unnecessary to describe in open court all the personal faults in your wife that would make her unsuitable as a custodial parent. A custody investigation would produce the same evidence, but it would be presented by an unbiased expert and would be confidential. (Both parents or their attorneys receive a copy of the report and recommendation shortly before the hearing.)

How Do Investigations Work?   To help the judge make a decision on custody, the investigative case worker obtains information from you and your wife about yourselves, any health or emotional problems either of you may have, your home and who lives in it, and general information about the child — his or her school, neighborhood, friends, and so on.

To obtain information from doctors and school authorities, you will be asked to sign release forms. Be sure you or your attorney finds out what information is being sought before you sign a release.

Frequently, the investigator will ask you and your wife to suggest witnesses who may have relevant information regarding your child and his or her welfare. Such witnesses may be professional persons (such as physicians, teachers, or psychiatrists) or simply people who know the child (such as the staff of a day-care center or babysitter).

Choose your witnesses with care. They should be people who are familiar with the child and have something substantial to say on your behalf. If you're unsure about what someone might say, suggest someone else.

At a home visit, the investigator will talk to you and your wife separately. Depending on the age of the children, they will be interviewed to find out their feelings regarding custody. The children should, of course, be neat and clean, but don't prepare them for the interview or attempt to persuade them to take your side. Just say who's coming and why.

Generally, you should answer the investigator's questions freely but without volunteering too much. Don't waste your time (and prejudice your case) by narrating your wife's sins and how lousy a parent she has been or will make. Remember again that, theoretically at least, the interviewer is only concerned with the best interests of the child — not which parent is the most or the least honorable.

You may find that the person interviewing you is hostile to you or biased against you. If so, control your anger and furnish the information requested. Make sure that all the information favorable to you is included in the report. Your lawyer will have an opportunity later to go over the report with you.

The Report and Recommendation The investigator writes out the report, including in it any written statements from the witnesses interviewed and a recommendation to the judge regarding custody. Judges are *not required* to follow these recommendations, but they may. Whether they actually give the reports and recommendations a lot of weight depends to a great extent on the confidence they have in the investigators.

Your lawyer is entitled to cross-examine your investigator as to the contents of the report and its general accuracy. Your lawyer may also show that the investigator is biased against you. In any event, leave the legal fireworks to the legal expert — don't try to pick apart the report yourself and impress everyone.

Help from Other Sources

Frequently, a father needs the help of a community agency or other professional service to help bolster his custody case. In most instances, of course, your lawyer will tell you when and why you need an expert witness.

In his divorce action, Jim seeks custody of his young son, who is emotionally disturbed. Jim is convinced that it would be detrimental to the boy for his mother to have custody.

Jim and fathers like him who need to consult an expert might try a private psychiatrist, the community child guidance clinic, the community mental health services, school guidance clinics, social workers, conciliation court personnel, the Family Service Association, or the Children's Home Society.

Preparing for a Trial or Hearing

Your lawyer should prepare you for the trial or hearing as time permits. But you'd be well advised to do what you can to help yourself. Many domestic relations lawyers have neither the time nor the inclination to do much more than go over the case one time the night before.

First and foremost, remember that in most states the judge will award custody on the basis of what he or she sees as the child's best interests. (Remember that Oklahoma and South Dakota are exceptions and follow the maternal preference rule.) This means that the judge should consider *all the evidence* (including your testimony, your wife's testimony, and the testimony of other persons) that is relevant to the issue of the child's best interests.

Your Private Life This is a poor time to be playing games in your private life — for a number of reasons. First, the judge is entitled to examine the living arrangements of you and your wife, since they are relevant to the best interests of the child. If your living arrangement might appear suspect to some people (such as the judge), why prejudice your case?

On the other hand, if you've been separated for some time,

have established a solid relationship with another woman, and are living with her, you should admit it and use it to your advantage. Don't try to show how "far-out" you are by insisting that everyone accept this arrangement, but don't apologize either. The judge will know the facts anyway, usually through the investigator's report.

Proof Required A father seeking custody of his children must, in most instances, be prepared to show in court at least the following:
- He will provide a stable home life for the children.
- He will spend sufficient time with the children to be a good parent to them.
- He is financially and emotionally able to be a custodial parent.
- He is seriously seeking to be a parent and not trying to avoid child support payments or to hurt his wife.
- He has made sufficient preparations to care for the children immediately.
- The environment of his home will enhance the best interests of the children, taking into account their ages, interests, background, and education.

In considering your fitness to be a custodial parent, the judge may also consider such things as your character, disposition, emotional stability, your neglect or indifference toward the child, your trustworthiness, as well as your acts and conduct.

Some judges may require more or less proof than others. And, of course, in a maternal preference state, the father must offer proof of the mother's unfitness to be the custodial parent.

Seeking Custody of Daughters Until fairly recently, most judges were reluctant to award the custody of a daughter to the father. It was generally assumed that single fathers were incompetent to deal with the problems of a growing female and her sexuality. Often this was probably true.

Studies have shown, however, that parental concern and anxiety concerning sex and sex education is not limited to men. Mothers share the same concern, but doubt themselves less. The most important thing to convince the judge of is that *you* are sexually secure. If so, you won't have too much of a problem. And if you do, get some help. Mothers do — all the time.

Your Ability to Maintain a Household These days, few judges will demand that you demonstrate your proficiency at making soup or changing diapers in order to be granted the custody of your children. If you lack confidence about your ability to run the house, don't worry about it. You'll learn. The point is: Are you a stable person who can handle stress? Your wife may be an expert in running the house but likely to fall apart under the demands of child-care.

The Trial or Hearing

Some strategies to help you survive court hearings generally are outlined in Chapter Seven, "Going to Court."

A custody trial or hearing may be either separate from or part of the divorce proceedings. A judge hears the case; there is no jury. In many domestic relations departments, these hearings are held in a closed courtroom; that is, the only persons allowed in are the parties, the witnesses, and the court personnel.

At the hearing, the judge must invite you and your ex-wife to present your respective arguments. In addition, he or she will inspect the investigator's report, which may or may not put you at a serious disadvantage. If necessary, your attorney may demand that the investigator appear in court to be cross-examined by your attorney about the contents and recommendations of the report.

If your children are old enough to understand the questions and answers involved, the judge will probably ask them how they feel about the decisions to be made, although some judges make it a practice not to ask such questions of children. As you might expect, the judge will give little weight to the opinions of a very young child (for example, under seven) but may well weigh heavily the stated preferences of a teenager.

Judges are greatly influenced by prior precedent; that is, previous cases where the issues and circumstances are similar to those to be decided. This legal principle puts a heavy burden on men, since in many states it is very difficult for them to come up with legal precedents for male custody.

But the judge hearing a child custody case has personal values, as do the rest of us. Many judges decide such cases on their "gut feelings" about the truth or falsity of the testimony of the husband or wife. Furthermore, judges are generally influenced by other custody cases they have heard and by their own background.

A father seeking custody of his children must always remember that every contested case of child custody must be decided *on its own merits.* You may have heard of this case or that case being decided a certain way by a certain judge — perhaps the one hearing your case. Never mind. *Your case is different and unique.* The judge must be persuaded that you are the most likely custodial parent for your child under the specific facts shown by the evidence.

Appointing an Attorney for the Child Some states have recently enacted laws providing for independent legal representation of the child where that seems to be in the child's best interests. Most of these states require that the lawyer's expenses and fee be shared either equally or in equitable proportions by the parents.

In Oregon the law makes the appointment of counsel for the child mandatory in divorce custody proceedings. In some other states the laws permit but do not require the judge to appoint a private lawyer for the child. Among these states are Arizona, California, Colorado, Connecticut, Iowa, Nebraska, Utah, and Vermont.

A few states (for example, Kentucky and Wisconsin) will appoint a guardian *ad litem* (a temporary guardian just for the purposes of the custody battle) or a "friend of the court" to represent the child.

Independent representation of a child is based on the idea that neither parent necessarily represents the child's best interests because of their biases. This may or may not be true, but in any event there's not much you can do about it except have your lawyer try to work with the child's lawyer (or representative) as far as possible.

The Decision: Custody Award

Decree or Judgment   The choices judges face in divorce proceedings, in respect to children, are: they may decide to alternate custody between the parents; they may order joint custody; they may assign sole legal custody to one parent, allowing the other visitation rights; they may award sole custody to one parent and deny visitation rights to the other; or they may award custody to a third party.

Appeal   If the decision has been adverse to you, your lawyer has the right of appeal. This is usually costly, though, and you must consider carefully what your chances are of having the judge's decision reversed. Obviously, your attorney (and your wallet) are your best guides here.

Changing the Decree or Judgment Later   At any time after the custody order or decree is issued, either party may request of the same court that the decree or judgment be modified; that is, that custody be awarded to the other person or a third person. The party applying for the change must show that the circumstances have changed and warrant a new decree.

13
Joint Custody

After seven years of marriage and two children, Walt and Linda have agreed to get a divorce. They have also agreed to remain full-time, committed parents to their two girls and to share financial, legal, and day-to-day responsibilities for them. As a result, they have sold their home and bought two condominiums in the same development. The girls will spend three days a week with Linda and four with Walt. The court approves this plan and orders joint physical and legal custody.

Joint custody provides a happy ending to the usually dismal story of parental divorce. Everyone is a winner, in theory. The parents get their divorce, and both are able to continue a meaningful and legal relationship with their children. The children, untraumatized by divorce or parental loss, joyfully walk off into the sunset with a different parent on different days.

This is a fashionable solution to the very real problem of child custody following parental divorce. Joint custody gives us what we all want. There are no bad people, no bad parents, and no losers. It is the ultimate in "no fault" divorce, equality, and rationality. Parents are conveniently free from blame, guilt, recrimination, sexism, loss of their child, and total responsibility for their child.

Well-intentioned parents can negotiate the details of joint custody without going through the legalities, regardless of how the custody and visitation orders read. For example, a father having custody of his son may allow the boy to live most of the week with his mother and return home on weekends. Thus, many of the practical benefits of joint custody seem illusory, since cooperation and mutual respect are necessary in any event.

However, there are philosophical and psychological benefits in joint custody. This arrangement provides recognition of each parent's equal need and ability to parent children, and the importance of both the father and the mother. Furthermore, fathers, who for the most part are the non-custodial parents, are given an equal negotiating position and an equal stake in their children.

Nevertheless, the real test of joint custody is *whether it works for the children*. Children are growing and dependent creatures. As well as meaningful relationships with their mothers and fathers, they need security and structure in their daily lives, discipline, and a family life with substance. Does joint custody meet children's needs? Or is it another example of parents assuming that what is convenient for them is also best for their children?

We don't claim to know the answer. Many so-called experts have opinions, but as yet these are only opinions. No long-term, widespread research has been done on joint custody. Certainly, many ex-spouses have developed or drifted into informal joint-custody-like arrangements. Many of these have been successful, or at least the most workable alternative. A small number of divorcing parents have been awarded joint custody orders. And apparently most have considered the joint custody experiment reasonably successful.

In our opinion, joint custody is unlikely to be *the* answer, or even one of the major answers, to the problems of child custody on a national scale. However, joint custody still may be the best alternative for some individual fathers, mothers, and children. For this reason we believe that the laws of all states should provide the option of joint physical and legal custody.

We suggest that you, if you are a father confronted with a custody decision, consider joint custody as an option. Custody questions should always be decided according to

what is best for each child and his or her mother and father —
not according to what is best in the usual case or in most
situations. Furthermore, joint custody is, by nature, tailored
differently to each family. You may want to include some,
but not all, aspects of joint custody in your custody agreement or court order.

Married parents, unless otherwise ordered by a court,
have joint physical and legal custody of their child. This
means that each parent has the right to decide the child's
education, religious training, place of residence, and so on,
and the obligation to support, care for, and discipline the
child. While each parent alone can do all of these things,
the law assumes that their parental rights and responsibilities
are exercised jointly.

Generally, a joint custody order following parental separation provides for a somewhat similar custody arrangement
to continue. There are, however, innumerable legal and
informal variations on the general joint custody theme.
So many, in fact, that you may decide not to bother.

In this section we discuss informal joint custody and
divided or *split custody*. Remember: these situations are
technically not joint custody. Both though, are frequently
confused with joint custody, and both provide many of the
benefits of joint custody.

Legal and Physical Custody

Child custody can be thought of as divided into two parts —
legal and *physical* custody. With legal custody comes the
right to make decisions for a child, to manage the child's
affairs, and to determine how he or she is reared. Physical
custody is the management and providing of daily child-care.
For example, a legal custodian decides which school a child
shall attend, while a physical custodian sees that a child gets
to school with a proper breakfast and clean clothes. Generally, a child's physical and legal custodians are the same;
that is, one or both of the parents.

Informal Joint Custody

Five years ago Maria and Joe were divorced, and Maria was awarded sole custody of their two children, Jason, then aged 10, and Julie, then aged 8. Through the years Maria and Joe have jointly made all major decisions concerning their children. Currently, Jason lives with his father but stays with his mother during his father's frequent business trips. Julie lives with her mother, but last year was in Joe's care during her mother's eight-week illness. Joe and Maria have negotiated changes in child support. All this has happened without ever going back to court or ever changing the original court order.

Over a period of time, most parents find that practicality and common sense become more important than court orders. A child needs to be with the non-custodial parent; it is arranged. Visitation needs to be longer or more frequent; it is arranged. Child support needs to be changed; it is.

The fact is, parents can arrange custody, visitation, and child support any way they wish, provided neither parent complains and a problem doesn't arise that causes the authorities to intervene. Courts don't look for cases to decide. They only decide questions when asked.

Sensible parents usually do exercise some degree of joint custody. That is, of course, at the discretion of the custodial parent. The custodial parent authorizes the non-custodial parent to confer with school teachers and to consent to medical treatment of the child in the custodial parent's absence. When major decisions or problems concerning the child arise, the non-custodial parent is consulted.

Informal joint custody has one major drawback — it's not legal joint custody. This means that the practical and fair arrangements that have been worked out can continue only with the approval of the custodial parent. Furthermore, the non-custodial parent is at a disadvantage from a legal standpoint. Without court approval, the child does not have the security of a permanent arrangement.

If you are a custodial father who has participated in a longstanding informal joint custody arrangement, we suggest that you make the arrangement legal. As you are likely to be the technical non-custodial parent, this court approval is particularly to your advantage. There are few reasons not to go ahead. You and your ex-spouse know that the arrangement can and does work. You have proven its practicality through time. A judge will have difficulty denying an existing way of operating that is benefiting your children.

Divided or Split Custody

Rob and Tim live with their mother, in California, during the school year. Their mother has physical and legal custody. During this time, their father pays child support. Come summer, the boys go to Washington and their father's care. Their father then has full legal and physical custody. And it's their mother's turn to pay child support.

Divided or split custody is a formal, court-ordered custody arrangement. The child is in the full legal and physical custody of the father for part of the year and in the full legal and physical custody of the mother for the rest of the year. Visitation and child support may also be included in the court order.

On the surface, the divided custody situation may appear like a sole custody/liberal visitation arrangement. *It is not.* A non-custodial parent who takes care of his or her child during a visitation period is not the child's legal custodian and is not entitled to make any major decisions concerning the child. However, a parent having divided custody is, during his or her custody period, *alone* entitled to make all major decisions regarding the child.

The courts are very reluctant to award divided custody, since they fear that it inordinately disrupts a child's life. Their reluctance also stems from the fact that the time span provisions of a divided custody order can be very difficult to change.

Note: Divided custody is also called *alternating custody.* Split custody sometimes refers to brothers and sisters who are placed in the custody of different parents.

Joint Legal Custody

Ron and his 16-year-old son, Alan, have set up housekeeping together. Although Ron is Alan's physical custodian, legal custody is shared by Ron and Sarah, Alan's mother. Sarah has equal rights with Ron to decide matters like Alan's schooling, his discipline, whether he can take a job as a camp counselor this summer, and whether he should get a driver's license. Should these parents decide to turn Alan loose on the highways, both will be responsible for any damage he might cause.

Joint legal custody simply means that each parent shares in the function of making parental decisions. The essence of this arrangement is that they continue to share equal responsibility and authority with respect to their children. Divided custody, by contrast, provides that each parent has authority and responsibility only during his or her period of custody.

This of course involves frequent consultation and agreement on all major decisions affecting the children and on all matters having a significant impact on the children's lives. Such matters may include education, religion, upbringing, and financial support. Also probably included are medical and psychological help, where appropriate, school vacations, and the like.

Each parent can legally make any of these decisions alone without consulting the other parent. For joint legal custody to be workable, it is essential that each parent trusts the other's judgment and each is willing to consult. Sarah, the mother described above, for example, has the right to send her 16-year-old son to a scuba-diving program without the father's approval.

Joint legal custody, not including joint physical custody, is often exactly what separating parents want. They want equal rights to decision making, but they also want their child to live primarily with one parent.

The courts, however, are very hesitant to split physical and legal custody. Even if you want joint legal custody only, you will probably have to buy the usual joint custody package — joint legal and physical custody. You and your child's other parent, then, can make the practical arrangements as you wish.

Joint Physical and Legal Custody

Alex and Leona are divorcing after 16 years of marriage and three children, aged 15, 14, and 12. Leona is a returning university student, and Alex continues to travel frequently on his job. Both parents believe that keeping their busy schedules and adequately caring for their active children are beyond the stamina of either one of them alone. They work out an agreement that provides for them to have joint legal custody – Leona to care for the children in her home four days a week and Alex to care for the children the remainder of the week.

Joint physical and legal custody, as in the example, is the popular and standard legal conception of joint custody following parental separation. The rest of this chapter deals with this type of joint custody.

This arrangement includes all the rights and responsibilities involved in joint legal custody and also provides that children live with each of their parents on a more or less equal basis. It differs from divided custody both in that legal custody is continuously shared and in that the parent actually caring for the child alternates frequently.

Alabama, Ohio, and Texas are the only states that specifically do not permit joint custody. California, Iowa, North Dakota, Oregon, and Wisconsin have explicitly made provision for joint custody awards following parental separation or divorce.

Practically speaking, there is no general rule for the mechanics of sharing physical custody of a child. Variations seem to depend on the parents' and the child's needs and what the courts will accept. Some parents and courts choose to spell out arrangements very specifically. For example: "Monday through Thursday Susie will be in her father's care. The remainder of the week she will be in her mother's care." Other court orders simply award joint custody and leave the parents and the child to work out the details.

When Joint Custody Won't Work   Before you begin to see yourself in a hypothetical joint custody situation, consider the following:

• You do not believe your child's mother exercises good

judgment, is trustworthy, or has an acceptable lifestyle.
- You do not believe your child's mother is a competent parent.
- Either you or your child's mother does not accept or want your separation.
- You had difficulties parenting before your separation.
- You do not believe your child needs frequent contact with his or her other parent.
- Your children, if they are old enough, do not want joint custody or are unwilling to accept the inconveniences of this arrangement.
- You and your child's mother are not equally committed to sharing the normal responsibilities of parenting, as well as the joys.

Any of the above statements, if applicable to your situation, is a good indication that joint custody will not work for you. This does not mean that either you or your child's mother is a bad parent, uncooperative, bitter, or sexist. It simply means that another custody arrangement will probably work better.

Benefits and Drawbacks of Joint Custody You and your child's mother may be in the best position to decide whether joint custody is the most workable alternative for both of you and your child. However, consider some of the advantages and disadvantages pointed out by the legal and psychological experts before you choose any of the legal custody options:

Drawbacks:
- The issue of custody is never resolved.
- The legal and emotional responsibility for a child is never pinned down.
- The relationship of parents who have decided to separate is allowed to continue.
- The child is given an unstable, inconsistent, and unstructured living environment that provides him or her with two sets of values.
- It is a sop to bolster the feelings of the parent who wouldn't have been awarded custody.

Benefits:
- Both parents are given an equal footing in deciding the welfare of their child.
- Both parents can remain involved in their child's daily life.
- The feelings of guilt and loss that usually follow a divorce are minimized for father, mother, and child.
- The equal importance of a mother and a father in a child's life is recognized.
- The daily responsibilities of child rearing can be shared by two parents.
- Parents are more likely to meet their support obligations and to remain involved in their child's life.
- This may be the only way a father can get custody of his child.

Joint Custody Agreements and Court Awards

You and your child's mother will need to agree to joint custody. Among the reasons why courts are reluctant to award joint custody is the belief that the differences and disagreements that caused the divorce will interfere with joint parenting. Parents who cannot agree both to the joint custody and to the practical aspects of such a situation will not be considered good candidates for legal co-parenting.

Furthermore, once you agree, you can expect to face considerable opposition to your plan. The first roadblock probably will be your lawyer. He or she may never have heard of joint custody and very likely will not understand it. Be prepared to hear that joint custody doesn't work and is unnecessary. Then you will be directed to choose one of two convenient legal pigeonholes: sole custody, mother; and sole custody, father.

You will, however, need a lawyer. Two organizations, NOW (National Organization for Women) and Equal Rights for Fathers, may be good referral sources for sympathetic and knowledgeable attorneys.

The second roadblock is the court. You and your child's mother may have agreed to joint custody, but the court will have to approve your agreement. Judges (and most lawyers) dislike joint custody. It offends their sense of order and the need for clearly defined responsibilities. They fear future disagreements between parents and imagine disputing parents later returning to court in order to decide whether junior should attend military academy or a free school.

Even if you can convince the judge that joint custody is practical and that you and your child's mother will be able to work out problems as they arise, you still must convince the court that joint custody is *in your child's best interests.* The court is likely to believe that you, as parents, are putting your own needs before your child's. The court will be concerned that joint custody may provide an unstable, totally unstructured home life for your child, one that will provide much parental contact but little consistency and discipline.

The result of all these roadblocks is that you and your child's mother must not only agree to joint custody, you, together, must be prepared to defend your proposal in court. Logistics, practicalities, and the reasons joint custody will benefit your child should be spelled out. A vague plea for an alternate lifestyle or for a novel form of custody will not convince the court.

Some of the specifics that you and your child's mother must work out are described in the following sections. What you agree to may be included in the marital settlement agreement and become part of the actual court order. Even if the details are omitted from the court custody order, however, we suggest that you put them in written form for your reference.

Flexibility   Some flexibility will be necessary in the agreement. This is true even when parents and children have lived with informal joint custody for years. Children and parents will have schedules and personal agendas that won't coincide with the letter of your agreement. For example, your daughter may want to play on a soccer team near her mother's home on a day she should be in your care.

New joint custody arrangements usually require a bit of practical working out. What seems like a great idea can be totally unworkable.

Flexibility is crucial because you must avoid having to go back to court to change details. Courts will not accept this type of bother.

Division of Time   Again, here, every situation is probably different. One mother and father agreed to have their daughter live during the school year with her mother and stay with her father, in another state, during her school vacations. Other parents decided that their children would stay in the father's care during working hours and the rest of the time with the mother. Another mother and father decided that their daughter would live three-and-a-half days a week with each parent.

Whatever the details your arrangement must give your children a reasonably predictable routine and environment. It should be clear which of you is in charge and when. Transportation details must also be worked out.

Child Support   Flexibility and fairness, as usual, are the name of the game. The amount of time each parent is responsible for the child, the relative earnings and expenses of both parents, the costs of transportation, and the needs of the children are all considerations. And all of these are apt to change. Furthermore, in the beginning, it is difficult to predict what the costs will be.

In joint custody situations, child support may be ordered by the court, agreed to informally, or dispensed with entirely. Remember, though, that expenses such as clothing, tuition, medical costs, and dancing lessons should be discussed and divided.

Be prepared to negotiate frequent changes. When you are married, the costs of rearing your child were not always predictable, and they may continue to be unpredictable in joint custody.

Moving and Taking the Child from the Area   Job offers, transfers, remarriage, and other personal considerations often make it difficult for parents to stay in the same area. This is true even for parents who are very committed to their children. While it is advisable for parents to plan to remain in the same area, one of them may need to move. You should include a provision for this in your agreement.

Usually, joint custody gives either parent the right to travel anywhere with the child. This means that your child's mother or you can legally take your child to another state and set up housekeeping. As a result, it is advisable to include a provision requiring the consent of both parents before the child can leave the state.

Consultation between Parents   Obviously, you will need to consult on all major concerns and decisions regarding your child. For example, Susie's progress in school, whether she should attend summer camp, and how to handle her experimentation with drugs will require both parents to confer. However, consultation can be just as important for the minor and everyday concerns. Susie's dental appointment, her history report due next Monday, and her bickering with her brother will all need to be followed up.

When the care of the children is alternated frequently, very regular consultation is crucial. Consistency of discipline and attention to daily problems and concerns are important. Children are often able to manipulate both parents, and they receive no effective guidance when this attention is lacking.

Resolving Disputes   You and your child's mother will have disputes. Even if you are cooperative, well-meaning, nice people this is likely to happen. You are still human.

Hopefully, you and your child's mother can agree, or at least, compromise. However, when consultation and negotiation fail, you may need another resource.

This matter can be brought to the court's attention, and the court will decide which parent's wishes should prevail. But, in the process, the judge will probably also decide that joint custody is a failure and award custody to one parent. We suggest that you and your child's mother provide that either counseling or arbitration be used first in order to avoid returning to court.

14
Child Support

Fathers never win in child support matters. Nor do mothers or children. The income that supported one household must now support two. The best to be hoped for is an arrangement that provides for equitable belt-tightening by yourself, your children's mother, and your children.

Remember: child support is for your children. You want them to be as well provided for as possible — the courts, in fact, will insist on this. The children's needs come first, and if you and their mother must make some sacrifices, then so be it.

Furthermore, if the child support award is unfair in your favor, it will only lead to more disagreement between you and your children's mother. You will have to continue some sort of relationship with your ex-partner, since she *is* your children's mother, and there is no sense in making unfair child support an ongoing issue. The best plan for all concerned is to be fair and businesslike.

We have mentioned in other chapters the trend toward "de-sexing" family law. Many states have theoretically adopted this policy in child support awards. Other states continue to hold that the father, rather than both parents, bears the responsibility of child support. However, we have emphasized the law of the "de-sexed" states in this book, since we believe that this is the future direction of family law.

In a similar vein, we have "de-sexed" this text. We do not assume that you will be paying child support; your children's mother may be paying it. Nor do we assume that you will earn more money or have more property than your children's mother.

What Is Child Support?

The term *child support*, as used in divorce proceedings, refers to the duty of one parent to pay his or her *share* of the continuing cost of maintaining and supporting the child after the parents end their relationship. Generally, the same obligations and legal procedures apply for unmarried parents.

The other parent, usually the custodial parent, also has a continuing duty to furnish his or her share of that cost. Frequently, in the heat of battle, one or both parents fails to remember that their *respective* obligations toward the child remain, no matter which of them is awarded custody of the child.

Sandy is ordered to pay Greg $200 per month child support for each of their two children. Greg, although he has custody of the children, still pays a share of their support. The expenses of his three-person household — food, house payment, children's clothing, day-care, medical care, recreation, and so on — amount to about $1,200 each month.

The obligation of child support is owed *to the child*, even though in most instances it is paid to the custodial parent. Both parents can be ordered to pay child support when their child is living with a third person.

What Are the Purposes of Child Support?

Child support payments are for the use and benefit of the *child*. The person receiving these payments on behalf of the child must use them like a trustee would; that is, he or she is liable if the funds are misused. Some of the things you can do to ensure that your child support payments are being used properly are discussed in this chapter.

Even though child support payments are for the use of the child, they will of course indirectly benefit the custodial parent by making his or her job easier. That parent, after all, must care for and feed the child on a daily basis whether any child support is received or not.

Don't fight a reasonable child support order or agreement because it may indirectly help your ex-wife if she is awarded custody of your child. *You are divorcing your wife, not your child.* And remember, child support orders are not chiseled in stone. They can always be changed later as the circumstances of the parents change.

Conversely, if you are awarded child custody and your ex-wife must make child support payments, your job is to protect the best interests of your child. How to do this is explained later.

Some Important Terms

Take a minute or two to acquaint yourself with the following definitions as they are used in child support problems:

changed circumstances — a new situation after divorce or separation that may justify raising or lowering the amount of child support

contempt — the legal result of disobeying a court order; may involve a fine, jail, or both

custodial parent — the parent having legal and physical custody of a child by agreement or court order

default — to be late in or miss a child support payment

interlocutory — temporary or interim, as in interlocutory child support order or interlocutory judgment

marital settlement agreement — a written contract providing for the rights and obligations of husband and wife following divorce or separation

modification — the changing, by lowering or raising, of a child support order or agreement

non-custodial parent — the parent not having legal or physical custody of a child

Who Pays?

Of all the maxims running back to the common law and before, a man's duty to support his children has been the most unquestioned — even by men.

However, the laws in many states now technically equalize the burden of child support and provide that fathers and mothers have equal duties of support, according to their circumstances.

This change is hardly surprising. Women have established their right to participate in the employment market, and men are no longer presumed to be the only breadwinners. Twice as many women work full-time as did in 1970. And of these, almost half (42 percent) support themselves and their families by working. Forty-five percent of these employed women plan to make their jobs a permanent career.

In practice, though, child support has not changed all that much. Fathers still bear the child support duties to a great extent, even though mothers may often be equally able to share this burden.

Equal Obligation of Mother and Father   In the states that have de-sexed their domestic relations laws, the parents have equal duties of child support. But even in the other states, if custody of a minor child is awarded to the father, the court has the power to order the mother to pay child support — depending of course on the circumstances.

Many attorneys and judges (and even parents) are loath to saddle a mother with child support, even though the circumstances clearly call for it. This is changing, though, and the courts are being forced to equalize child support awards on a more realistic basis.

Child Support to Custodial Parent   In most instances, child support is given by the non-custodial parent to the custodial parent. The amount of this support always depends on the circumstances of everyone concerned. Thus, in circumstances that do not warrant child support by the non-custodial parent, the court should not order any.

At the time Fred divorced his wife, he was an engineer making $45,000 a year. His wife was a clerk with an income of $600 a month. When Fred was awarded custody of the children, his wife was not required to pay child support.

Child Support Orders by Agreement

You and your wife may agree in writing on who is to pay child support and the amount of the payments. This agreement is usually part of the marital settlement agreement.

Note, however, that a judge is not bound by an agreement between you and your wife as to the amount to be paid in child support. Although you or your wife may agree to waive your right to alimony, you may not legally deprive a judge of his or her authority to award a suitable amount for the support of minor children.

Unmarried Parents Unmarried parents often make informal arrangements in regard to custody and child support and never feel the necessity of involving the court. We advise you to resolve these matters in court to avoid misunderstandings in the future, affirm your child's right to support, and establish your rights and responsibilities as a father.

Increasingly, unmarried parents are handling child support problems by making living-together contracts before their child's birth, and, should they separate, making support agreements similar to those made by married parents. However, not all states recognize living-together contracts. In those states which do not, child support obligations that are fair to the child will be enforced.

Understanding the Agreement It is preferable, of course, to work out a child support agreement before court proceedings, when you are calm and can talk with your lawyer freely. Both attorneys, together with their clients, can take their time reviewing the financial data that will determine child support and hopefully work out any minor disagreements.

Still, there is nothing wrong with a child support settlement made in court provided:
- Both parents clearly understand each term of the agreement.
- The agreement is fair to the child and both parents.
- The person being obligated to pay the child support will be able to fulfill the obligation.

217

Court Procedure

We advise you to use an attorney any time child custody or child support is an issue. Child support is a complicated, longstanding, and important matter. Even if you and your child's mother agree, the protection of having an attorney is worth the extra money involved.

Temporary Order   The judge issues this first support order on the basis of financial statements made by the parent requesting child support. These orders are effective as soon as they are received by the other parent. Remember, if you are ordered to pay an amount that seems unfair, you may ask the court to review the order.

Interlocutory Order   The first court hearing on the divorce case is usually called the "interlocutory" hearing. At this hearing the judge will make an interlocutory child support order after hearing both sides and the arguments. If a temporary child support order was obtained earlier, the interlocutory order replaces it.

This first interlocutory hearing is extremely important even though it is not final. Orders made during this hearing generally become final automatically, so you will want to give it your best shot at the interlocutory hearing.

"Final" Order   We use *final* in quotes because in a very important sense a child support order is *not* final until the child is of age or has been emancipated.

Interlocutory orders generally become final within a given period of time after the interlocutory hearing. *Final* means that the court makes its final judgment of divorce, and the parents are then legally divorced and free to remarry.

Determining the Amount of Child Support

The considerations determining a fair child support award should be pretty much the same no matter who is ordered to pay. These considerations, which are outlined later, are affected to some degree by the amount of spousal support (alimony) awarded, if any. That's because spousal support, of course, is a part of the circumstances of the party receiving it. And the circumstances of everyone, including the child, determine the amount of child support awarded.

Most of the lawbooks and lawyers say that there is no fixed formula or rule to determine the amount of child support a judge will order. In many states and in many courts in a given state that is true; each case is decided on its own facts and circumstances.

Nevertheless, judges have developed their own methods of shortcutting the mass of financial information that is usually thrown at them. This involves the use of tables that look very much like the IRS tax chart you use to figure out your income tax. If your court uses such charts, the clerk will furnish you with one.

These charts are not the Ten Commandments. You *can* offer evidence to the judge as to why he or she shouldn't use a chart, but your evidence had better be persuasive!

In courts that don't use these charts, the general criteria used for making a child support order are:
- the financial resources of the child
- the financial resources of the custodial parent
- the financial resources of the non-custodial parent (the one paying support)
- the standard of living enjoyed by the family and child
- the age and health of both parents
- the physical, emotional, and educational needs of the child

Note that the question of who is at fault (in those states still requiring fault for divorce) has no legal bearing on the amount to be awarded in child support. Still, if you have been keeping a gorgeous mistress somewhere and are unrepentant, it won't exactly help your case.

Word of warning: A judge can't make a child support order higher than it should be in order to make up for an alimony award he or she feels is too low. If this happens, your attorney should appeal the order.

Most of the above criteria are self-explanatory and can be

219

proved by such items as IRS returns, bank books, stock certificates, property tax statements or appraisals, bills, and canceled checks. And, of course, at the court hearing you may testify as to any of these matters. As in alimony obligations, debts of each or both parents are relevant to the issue of ability to pay child support.

The Needs of the Child   This item is often the most difficult to resolve. Does it mean membership in the tennis club? Cosmetic orthodonture? A college education? Most judges interpret the law to mean that the child should be provided with "necessaries" insofar as possible, which usually include:
  • suitable food, housing, furniture, and clothing
  • medicine and medical care and attention
  • means of education
  • social opportunity and protection
Again, what is necessary in each instance must be determined by the facts of each case, taking into account the resources of each parent and his or her abilities, social position, and circumstance.

The Person Charged with Support   The following will be considered by the judge in regard to the person who must pay support:
  • the amount of annual income
  • the extent to which the person is capable of increasing that income
  • the size of the person's estate
  • the person's age
  • the person's reasonable needs
  • the person's obligations with respect to alimony
  • the expenses to be incurred in supporting other children in the person's custody

Extraordinary Expenses   In most states, the non-custodial parent cannot be held liable for extraordinary expenses arising while the children are in the other parent's custody. The way that some judges deal with this general rule is by ordering the payment of expenses such as medical and dental treatment, education, and even vacations, in addition to the monthly support payments.

Children's Income   Parents who implant the work ethic in their kids reap the rewards. Should your child be an ambitious youngster, his or her earnings may lessen your support obligations. More likely, however, is that your child might have trust income. This can be used to reduce the parents' support payments.

Services in Lieu of Money   In some instances it may be feasible for you and your ex-partner to agree that you will render services in lieu of paying child support in money. What services can be considered support depends on the creativity of you and your child's mother and the court's opinion of what is fair to the child.

Hamilton, a bookish fellow who never made it on campus, worked at a quality bookstore for a non-quality wage. His wife, Tara, had truly made it. She had an outstanding voice and was in demand on the concert circuit. Their divergent interests drew them apart, but in common they had their love of their children. She wanted a divorce; he agreed.

Together they saw a traditional lawyer, and all took for granted that the wife would have custody. The lawyer, in spite of his disapproval, respected their mutually agreed-upon plans for child support and visitation. In lieu of support payments, the father would stay with the children in the mother's apartment while she was on tour or was otherwise absent. Their divorce order contained this arrangement.

Inflation Provisions: "Future" Income   Child support orders routinely include a clause that support be raised in accordance with inflation. Courts also have ordered child support based on a percentage of a parent's net compensation after taxes. Child support orders of this kind free parents from continually returning to court when the cost of living or their income changes.

When the Mother Has Means   The mother's earnings and sometimes her worldly riches can be used to support her

221

children. The courts have been unpredictable, though, and are often reluctant to compel a mother to use her property for the support of her children. Consider the following:

Jane was a registered nurse but unemployed. She filed for divorce and had two minor children. The stocks she owned were non-income stocks but very valuable. A temporary child support order in her favor was upheld on the ground that she was not required to sell the stocks.

The result may have been different, however, if her fortune had been derived from property that was readily salable or came from wage income. And, the mere fact that someone is wealthy does not, of itself, mean that he or she must pay child support.

In New York, Mrs. H. divorced her husband, who was a physician. Mrs. H. had a fairly large fortune of her own but filed for child support. Her request was denied on the basis that she failed to show the required necessity.

Which Method of Payment Should You Use?

Child support obligations need not always be paid in so many dollars per month. You and your children's mother have certain choices about how to meet support obligations. What you choose should depend on the needs of both of you and of your child — not on what is usually done. For the purpose of simplicity alone, we will assume in this section that the father is the parent charged with support.

Monthly Payments to Custodial Parent   This is the usual method ordered by judges unless the parties agree otherwise. It is often the easiest and most convenient method. A basis is set for a clear-cut, businesslike relationship between you and your ex-partner, and your respective finances are separate.

However, this may not be the method you choose if you want daily contact with your children or if you doubt your ex-partner's ability to manage money or your children.

Alternatives to Monthly Payments   Here are some other items that are commonly part of child support orders:

- mortgage payments
- property taxes
- homeowner's insurance, repairs, and maintenance
- fuel and utility bills
- medical, dental, and educational expenses
- vacations
- day-care
- trust for college education

Paying these expenses directly will assure you that your children's needs are being met, as well as give you some control over their daily lives. It may also give you a headache. Divorced fathers who pay child support in this manner often end up "husbanding" their ex-wives' business affairs.

If you doubt that your children's mother can manage money or care for your children, you should face the issue head on. You have a *custody* problem, not a child support problem.

However, do not mistake lack of experience for incompetence. Most people who have never paid a bill in their lives learn how to handle their business affairs quickly after a divorce.

A person who is too incompetent or untrustworthy to manage a household should not be responsible for the daily care of your children. They deserve better. Even though it may not suit your plans, you may need to become the custodial parent. However, if you lose a custody fight, then you and your attorney can devise ways of ensuring that child support goes to meet the needs of your children.

Paying through a Third Party   Often child support payments are paid through a public agency, the district attorney's office, or the welfare department (particularly if welfare is involved). *Our advice:* Avoid this at almost any cost. You will probably be treated impersonally, unsympathetically, and curtly. Your children may come to believe that the government, rather than you, is supporting them.

If your children's mother or the court insists on such a method, offer to do the same thing but through a bank.

Security for Payment   Although a judge cannot give away any part of your property to your children, the court may secure your child support obligation by requiring that your property be held in trust. A more usual practice is for the court to require the support-paying parent to maintain a life insurance policy with the child as beneficiary.

Your Child's College Education   In most cases, child support obligations end when a child reaches the age of majority, 18 or 21. This may leave your child still at Harvard without daddy to pay the bill. As a result, many child support agreements provide for support to continue until a child finishes his or her education, or for insurance or a trust for this purpose.

Income Tax Considerations

Unlike alimony, child support is not deductible from the gross earnings of the parent paying support. That parent can, however, claim the child as a dependent in most instances. This can be done either by agreement with the custodial parent or by fulfilling the tax law requisites for claiming dependents.

   If you and your former partner are careful about the tax consequences of your agreement and live in a state where spousal and child support can be lumped together in one award, you can both profit from it.

Steve grosses $20,000 a year. His ex-wife has no income. Steve pays $11,000 a year in child support. He claims himself and his two expensive children as exemptions and winds up paying the IRS $3,227 in taxes each year.

Alan also grosses $20,000 a year. He pays his ex-wife $11,000 a year in alimony. He claims only himself as a dependent but pays a tax bill each year of $1,007. His ex-wife claims herself and the two kids and pays $1,035. The IRS is $1,185 poorer. Dynamite!

   Be sure to discuss the specifics of your tax situation with your ex-wife and your attorney. Make sure that both of you understand the agreement and its consequences.

Failure to Pay Child Support

Ron tires of paying child support and decides to support his motorcycle instead. After months of nagging, pleading, and demanding, his ex-wife hauls him into court. And Ron winds up in Stony Lonesome.

We won't waste much time on this character. Parents do wind up in jail when they "willfully and deliberately" disobey court orders. In this case, the court order was for child support, and this is called criminal contempt. Ron had no lawful excuse for not supporting his children. In the end, he will have to pay back support, his normal obligations, and attorney's fees.

Charlie was ordered to pay $200 to his ex-wife for child support. He was a union carpenter at that time making $2,000 a month, but since January he had been laid off. He was four months in default on his child support payments when he was hauled off to jail.

Charlie may be hitting the bricks again looking for work after the judge hears the circumstances. Charlie could have saved himself some misery by contacting his former wife and explaining the circumstances or, if she wouldn't listen, going to court (without an attorney) and explaining to the judge what had happened. A man's lack of ability or means of child support is always a good defense.

But remember that none of the following will get you off the hook:

- Someone else is supporting the child.
- You aren't working because you quit your job or refuse to look for work.
- Your obligation has been transferred to someone else.
- You have failed to pay because you have other debts, including the obligation to help your parents.

Assignment of Wages   Partly because of the great number of parents who fail to fulfill their child support obligations, many states are stricter than they used to be in enforcing such laws. In California, for example, if you are an absent parent who is more than two months behind in your child support payments, your ex-spouse has a quick and effective remedy. He or she can apply to the judge for an order assigning your wages for this obligation. In other words, your employer must pay child support directly to your former spouse or someone acting on his or her behalf. Furthermore, many states have begun to cooperate more closely in collecting child support from people who have moved to other states.

15
Visitation

Saturday, 10 a.m. sharp, Dave arrives at the house he doesn't live in anymore. He braves the glare of his ex-wife, the sleepy look of her new friend, and then leaves with his five- and seven-year-old daughters. Dave has begun his long-awaited custody weekend.

The girls give him a run for his money — hamburgers, then the park, his mother's for some relief, dinner, a movie, bedtime stories, a guilty call to his girlfriend, cries in the night, cartoons at 7 a.m., and out to breakfast.

An exhausted Dave wonders how he'll entertain the girls for the next six hours and forty-five minutes of their weekend together.

The weekend father has become the most comic cartoon in the Sunday funnies; he has upstaged Dagwood. Deprived of meaningful contact with his children, he usually tries to compensate by being a perpetual jolly playmate or a Santa Claus trying to buy their affection.

No one is fooled. The weekend father feels uncomfortable and knows he tries too hard. His children also know this and are often unruly and manipulative. And the mother knows that her kids come home like a pack of wild animals after a visit with their father. Everyone realizes that this type of contact with children is, at best, superficial.

The legal right of visitation is a sop and a carrot. The sop: a father is given visitation rights after he has lost the right of custody. The carrot: the father earns the right of visitation by paying child support and cooperating with the child's mother. This practice ignores the most important function of visitation by the non-custodial parent — the maintenance of the relationship between parent and child.

A non-custodial parent need not be a laughable stereotype. Obviously, such a parent will spend less time with his or her children than is ideal, but the time spent *can* be a significant part of both their lives.

To accomplish this:

- Fathers must accept their importance to their children.
- Fathers must accept many of the ordinary difficulties of parenting and give up the fun and games, where appropriate.
- The courts must support creative, flexible visitation programs in which fathers have frequent but significant contact with their children.
- The custodial parent (usually the mother) must be prevented from frustrating or sabotaging the father's visitation rights.
- Both parents must cooperate to solve the numberless day-to-day problems that may arise, keeping in mind the paramount concern — the best interests of the child.
- Neither parent should use visitation as a weapon or as a shield.

The Law

Visitation by Agreement The best visitation agreements are generally worked out and agreed to by both parents. But even when the parents make such an agreement, the judge hearing the divorce case must approve it.

The judge will be guided by what appears to be in the best interests of the child. Normally, visitation agreements will be approved if they appear to be reasonable on the face of things and protect everyone's rights. On occasion, however, a judge will not approve the agreement and will deny visitation rights to the non-custodial parent for reasons we will examine later in this chapter.

Visitation by Court Order Court orders granting visitation are usually made in connection with hearings on other issues such as custody proceedings and child or spousal support.

Visitation orders are of two kinds. The first grants the

non-custodial parent "reasonable" visitation rights; the following is a typical example:

IT IS FURTHER ORDERED, ADJUDGED AND DECREED, that the care, custody, and control of the minor children born of this marriage should be awarded to the Petitioner, with the Respondent having reasonable visitation of such children upon reasonable advance notice.

The second kind of order spells out in detail the non-custodial parent's visitation rights; that is, the specific times, places, and conditions of the visitations.

Your considerations in deciding whether to try for a "reasonable" visitation order or a more specific one are discussed later in this chapter.

Persons Entitled to Visitation Visitation must be granted to the non-custodial parent unless it would be contrary to the best interests of the child.

In most states, visitation may also be granted to any person who has an interest in the child's welfare, for example, step-parents and grandparents.

How about *unmarried* fathers? A number of states (for example, California and New York) have recently allowed visitation rights to unmarried fathers — provided the best interests of the child are being met. This is in line with the expanding rights of unmarried fathers generally.

Traditional law declared that grandparents had no legal right to visitation with their grandchildren if the custodial parent or parents objected. The same was true if a stepparent with custody of the child objected.

The reasoning behind this old law was that, where animosity or hostility existed between the custodial parent or stepparent and the grandparents, the best interests of the child would not be served by such visitation. Furthermore, went the reasoning, the custodial parent's rights had precedence over the rights of persons more distantly related to the child.

Jim's father and mother helped Jim and his wife to care for their children and took a personal interest in them. When Jim and his wife separated, Jim's parents boarded the kids and parented them until the divorce was final. Jim's wife was awarded custody of the children and now objects to their grandparents seeing them.

Recently, almost twenty states (listed below) have enacted laws under which a grandparent may seek and obtain visitation with his or her grandchildren under certain circumstances. These circumstances usually involve the death of one or both of the child's parents or their divorce or separation.

Arkansas	Iowa	New York
California	Kentucky	Ohio
Connecticut	Louisiana	Oklahoma
Florida	Michigan	Texas
Georgia	Missouri	Utah
Hawaii	New Jersey	Wisconsin
Idaho		

Pete's parents have been a part of the lives of Pete's two children. When Pete was divorced, his wife received custody of the children, but the judge gave Pete's parents visitation rights. Pete's wife remarried, and the children were legally adopted by her new husband. Pete's parents wonder if that spells the end of their visitation rights.

In most states, when a grandparent has been granted visitation rights and the child is adopted by a stepparent, the adoption does not necessarily terminate the grandparent's visitation rights.

The result may be diferent, though, when a child is adopted by a person other than a stepparent. Check with your lawyer if you want more specific information on this problem.

If you are a grandfather with a visitation problem or a father who wishes to have your parents maintain contact with your children, you'll probably need the help of an attorney. Or you might try the Equal Rights for Fathers organization (check the white pages in your telephone book). Legal Aid may be of some help, depending on the quality of the organization in your area.

Visitation after Change in Custody

The custody of Roger's kids was given to his wife when they were divorced. Later, Roger successfully regained custody of the children on the grounds of their mother's neglect and abandonment. Now Roger's wife wants to visit the kids regularly.

The judge will, in all probability, grant Roger's wife reasonable visitation at the same time he makes the order changing custody. However, Roger can fight the visitation order if he feels visitation by his former wife would be detrimental to the children's best interests.

Visitation after the Court Order In the great majority of cases, the original court order ends the proceeding as far as the court is concerned. Generally, particularly after some time has passed, both parents live with one arrangement or another and the children are permitted to visit the non-custodial parent when he or she wishes.

On the other hand, many visitation disputes wind up back in court. Usually this is because one parent (or both) feels the judge has been unfair or because he or she is so angry with the other parent that harassing him or her seems worth it — it's not.

When visitation problems do wind up again before the judge, he or she may:
- lecture the offending parent
- punish the offending parent with a loss of support money, where appropriate
- hold the offending party in contempt for refusal to obey the order
- order a change in custody if the conduct is really reprehensible.

"Reasonable Visitation" vs. Specific Orders

Before deciding whether to seek reasonable visitation rights or specific visitation rights, you should have some idea of what judges and lawyers mean when they say "reasonable."

The laws of virtually every state fail to make clear exactly what reasonable visitation rights are. They are defined by each individual judge, usually by making a ruling on what "reasonable" means when one of the parents comes back into court with a complaint. Generally, though, "reasonable" translates into one or two weekends per month, a couple of weeks in the summer, and a special day or two such as every other Christmas or birthday.

Granted, "reasonable" sounds like legalese. What is reasonable to a mother may be insufficient to a father and unbearable to a child. The ultimate test, though, of what is reasonable is the judge's view of the best interests of the child.

What Kind of Order Should You Try to Get?   A visitation order or arrangement should be specifically framed to reflect the father's circumstances and the degree of his commitment to his children's lives and to his and the mother's schedules. But most importantly, visitation must meet the child's needs at a given time.

To a great extent, the advantages or disadvantages of reasonable visitation rights versus specific rights will be determined by how well or how badly you and your former wife handle your feelings. If it appears that you will invariably be at sword's point, you're probably better off with a specific order. On the other hand, after the heat of battle subsides, if you are able to agree with your wife as to what is best for everyone concerned, a flexible visitation order may suit you best.

If you have a job that frequently requires weekend work at short notice or vacations that cannot be planned in advance, a specific visitation order may cause you problems. However, you may be comfortable with such an order if you work regular hours and have regular vacation periods. In any event, always remember the distance you must travel to see the children.

Age of Child   The age of your child is a very important factor in arranging visitation. Obviously, visiting a two-month-old infant is very different than a teenager. A young child needs frequent and regular contact if the non-custodial parent wants to maintain a significant relationship with him or her. Also, a very young child will not tolerate an extended visit away from the custodial parent. And it may be questionable whether you could cope with a young infant for a long period, particularly if your work involves travel.

However, a reasonable visitation order may well suit the needs of a teenager who might resent having to spend weekends with you but enjoy spending an entire summer in your company.

Items to Include If you decide that specific visitation rights are for you, be advised that you should try for almost any arrangement that will sound reasonable to a judge in light of the circumstances. Here are some useful provisions that are commonly included in specific visitation orders:
- alternate weekends
- birthday, all or part of Christmas, Easter, Thanksgiving, and other holidays
- one or two weekday evenings
- lunch or daytime visits
- telephone contact
- during every several months, one additional, flexible visit

Some Practicalities

Court-ordered visitation may be a useful tool for several years following the parents' separation. For example, it may provide a structure for ex-partners to cooperate in the aftermath of a failed relationship.

But visitation can be a constant source of friction between you and your former wife and can provide a handy vehicle for either or both of you to get back at the other. The problem is that your child will pay a heavier price than either of you for any cheap shots you take at one another.

However, through the years, court visitation orders often become irrelevant or only a guide. Usually both parents and the child develop informal visitation arrangements that are flexible and better meet everyone's needs.

A major priority for the non-custodial father should be establishing the basis for flexible, cooperative visitation arrangements.

233

Here are some ways to make this happen:
• Demonstrate your commitment to remain in your child's life.
• Visit and telephone regularly.
• Be prompt and follow through on visitation plans.
• Change your plans only in the event of very unusual circumstances, and then give as much advance notice as possible.
• Within limits, be ready to change your plans to suit the convenience of your child and his or her mother.
• Discipline your child when appropriate.
• Offer to assume responsibilities, such as taking the child to dental appointments, staying home when the child is ill, and the like.
• During visitation, be yourself and expose your child to your normal life. Don't make every visit a treat.

When You or Your Ex-Partner Cannot Follow the Visitation Schedule   When your visitation rights have been fixed by a court order or by written agreement, there may be a number of situations where the schedule simply cannot be followed — due to no one's fault. For example, when your visitation is scheduled, the child may be ill. If so, the mother should permit you to visit the child in bed — or at home — as the case may be.

Suppose your ex-wife wants to take your child to a school party at the time your visitation is scheduled. She should obtain your consent, and another time and place can be scheduled to replace the missed visit. On the other hand, if you want to take your child to the circus when no visit is scheduled, you should obtain the consent of your ex-wife.

In the event that you and your ex-wife cannot agree on such substitutions of visitation, each of you should make the best of it and forego the event.

Don't Dump Your Child with a Sitter   Many men insist on their visitation rights merely to spite their wives. When they pick up their kids, they dump them with a girlfriend or parent to have their time to themselves without being bothered. Most marital settlement agreements prohibit this. Even if yours doesn't, don't do it.

Petty Harassment

According to court order, Floyd can visit his five-year-old daughter, Tammy, alternate Saturdays from nine to six. Floyd has arrived promptly for the last three visits and found Tammy "ill" once and still in her nightgown twice. Today, he finds that she has no clean clothes.

Our advice to Floyd: grin and bear it. Floyd, like many newly divorced fathers, finds his ex-wife using visitation as a vehicle to continue the fights of their past marriage. After a period of time, most ex-wives (and ex-husbands) discover petty harassment is boring and not worth their time. Should his ex-wife persist in this behavior, there is little that Floyd can actually do. At best, he can haul her into court for a well deserved lecture.

When May Visitation Be Denied or Stopped?

Visitation by a parent may be denied at the time the custody order is made by the judge, or, when visitation is granted, it may be withdrawn on a showing that it is contrary to the best interests of the child. Generally, the same reasons exist in either case.

Visitation is denied only under extraordinary circumstances. Often a parent who would never be given custody of a child is given the right of visitation. For example:

Sam plays the fiddle all summer and begs for his dinner come winter. Debbie, his ex-wife, grew tired of being both the breadwinner and the breadbaker, divorced her ne'er-do-well husband, and was awarded custody of their two daughters. Sam, provided the sun is shining, has the right to visit his daughters.

Grounds for Denial or Discontinuation of Visitation Visitation rights may be denied or discontinued on the basis of the same sort of mental, moral, or emotional defects that influence the decision to deny custody to a parent. Examples of such grounds are a likelihood that the parent in question will physically harm the child, is mentally or physically incompetent, will have a harmful emotional effect on the child, or will subject it to an improper and immoral atmosphere. Similarly, the likelihood of "alienation of affection" (sabotaging the child's regard for the other parent) often also influences a court to deny visitation rights.

State laws usually make specific provisions for the denial of visitation to the non-custodial parent. The following are the usual grounds:

Relating to the Welfare of the Child:
- visitation causes an emotional and nervous condition
- visitation affects the physical health of the child adversely
- the mental illness of the parent causes trauma to the child
- the child is unwilling to visit or visitation causes fear in the child

Relating to the Conduct of the Parent:
- indecency or adultery of the parent
- immoral conduct toward the child
- drunkenness or use of drugs
- criminal activities
- cruelty; neglect of the child
- abandonment of the child — failure to visit
- nonsupport of the child or failure to pay spousal support
- unauthorized removal of the child from the jurisdiction of the court
- alienation of affection (sabotaging the child's regard for the other parent)

Other Grounds:
- religious conflicts causing harm to the child
- the wishes of the stepparent

Warning: Seldom is visitation denied on any *one* of the above grounds. Almost always a combination of these circumstances influences a judge to deny visitation. In short, even when one or more of these grounds exist, a judge will always consider *all the circumstances*.

Denying Visitation Because of Non-Payment of Support

Unfortunately, non-payment of support remains one of the major reasons fathers are denied visitation or have difficulty arranging visitation with their child's mother. A father's right of visitation is one of the few incentives available to mothers, district attorneys, and welfare departments to get unwilling fathers to support their children.

Generally, though, unless the state in which the father lives has a specific law stating otherwise, his visitation rights may not be withheld or denied just because he failed to pay spousal or child support.

Denying a parent's visitation rights deprives the child of the parent's necessary company during the formative years of childhood. Frequently the only practical result is that the child will be deprived both of the support payments and of the parent's company. Furthermore, non-support may be the result of many circumstances besides deliberate refusal and irresponsibility.

But if you have made an agreement with your wife in which visitation rights are conditioned upon your payment of support, the courts will generally hold that the mother has no obligation to permit visitation if you are in default. On the other hand, if the marital settlement agreement provides for both visitation and payment but does not make one conditional upon the other, you have a much better chance of avoiding denial of your visitation rights. (The same is generally true of nonpayment of spousal support.)

If your visitation rights have been threatened because of non-support, you can frequently receive help through what lawyers call "expert testimony." This may include opinions favorable to you from such sources as welfare agencies, court investigators, domestic relations investigators, court welfare workers, probation officers, juvenile officers, departments of public assistance, departments of domestic conciliation, police departments, departments of public welfare, friends of the court, and the like.

Fathers *can* avoid this entire issue. When, through no fault of their own, they are unable to meet their child support obligations, they can ask the court to change the support order.

Warning: Fathers who are unfairly prohibited from visiting their children are often tempted to withhold child support. By doing this they may give their child's mother legitimate grounds for denying visitation. *Don't do this*. See your lawyer instead!

When Visitation Rights Are Not Exercised   As a general rule, if the non-custodial parent has failed to exercise his or her visitation rights for a substantial period of time, that alone does not necessarily justify denial of visitation rights.

However, in many cases visitation rights are terminated if the non-custodial parent failed to visit the children for a sufficient period of time. The following are examples of this rule:

- Pennsylvania (mother had seen children twice in seven years)
- Illinois (mother had visited children twice in nine years)
- Delaware (mother hadn't visited children since divorce two years before)
- New York (wife hadn't visited children at all in more than eight years)

In most of these cases, the sole fact of non-visitation was seldom the reason the courts terminated visitation rights. In most instances, the non-custodial parent's conduct was also a factor in the court's decision (such as living in open adultery while not visiting the child).

Immoral Conduct and Sexual Activities

Charlie has visitation rights with Susan, his twelve-year-old daughter. Charlie has lived with another woman for several years and has a stable relationship with her, but they are unmarried. Charlie's former wife asks the court for an order prohibiting Charlie from taking Susan to his home or, alternatively, stopping his visitation rights. As grounds, Charlie's wife alleges that the conduct of Charlie and his girlfriend is harmful to Susan.

Generally, private sexual activities do not constitute good grounds for denial or termination of visitation rights unless the custodial parent can show they have a harmful effect on the child. In short, as long as the visiting parent conducts himself or herself properly in the presence of the child, visitation will be permitted. In the example given above, the judge would probably deny the request of Charlie's ex-wife in the absence of any proof that the conduct of Charlie and his partner was harmful to Susan.

John was awarded custody of his daughter, aged nine, and his son, aged thirteen. He lives in a small community noted for its religious beliefs. John's wife, during a visitation, takes the children to public places along with her latest boyfriend, with whom she has lived for a week. The kids tell John they are embarrassed, and the other kids taunt them about their mother. Their school grades fall off.

John may be successful in terminating his former wife's visitation rights, or at least in getting a court order forbidding her to visit the children in the company of her latest lover. Again, though, the courts are very reluctant to terminate visitation rights completely, and John will probably have to call in school personnel or psychologists to bolster his case.

If the conduct of your former wife is patently outrageous, you will have little problem terminating her visitation rights or requesting a change of custody. Most "conduct" cases, though, are very close calls.

When in doubt, play it safe. If you're the visiting parent and your former wife is upset over your social life, forget the girlfriend for a while until you return the kids. But if you *know* your conduct is O.K. and feel your ex-wife is just harassing you, go get a court ruling and settle the matter once and for all.

What to Do If Visitation Is Denied   If you have been denied visitation, or fear you might be, it is often possible to offer either to have your visitation supervised (by a court social worker, for example) or to have it occur at a given time and place.

Remember also that visitation orders are not permanent in the sense that they cannot be changed. If you were denied visitation but your situation has improved and you feel you now have a better case, you can apply to have the order changed.

What to Do If Visitation Is Frustrated or Sabotaged

In April, Matt is scheduled to have his daughter, Betty, for the weekend. The day before his visitation, his ex-wife calls and tells him Betty doesn't feel well.

In May, when Matt arrives for his visitation, he finds a note tacked on the door signed by his ex-wife telling him she and Betty unexpectedly had to visit grandma for the weekend.

In June, Matt is about ready to go bananas when, the week before his visitation weekend, his ex-wife tells him she's arranged for Betty to go to summer camp during that period. After all, she says, doesn't Matt want the best for his little girl?

In July, Matt sees his lawyer.

Visitation lends itself to manipulation because its enforcement, on a day-to-day basis, depends on the cooperation of the father and mother. Your former spouse's threat of reducing your precious time with your kids is a very effective weapon to use against you.

However, a parent may seek to reduce or stop visitation by the other parent for valid reasons that may be in the best interests of the child. Often a parent will attempt to do this on his or her own without a court order. This is a dangerous practice since, in many states, deliberate violations of visitation orders are grounds for a change in custody.

The litany of methods by which your visitation rights may be frustrated or blocked is endless and depends only on the ingenuity of your former wife. If this is happening to you, keep a careful record of each incident, the reason given for it, and what you did about it. The judge will look for a *pattern* of such behavior, not isolated incidents. And while you're doing it, try to keep your temper.

Depending on where you live, if your former spouse has frustrated or blocked your visitation rights, your lawyer may ask the judge to:

- change the original visitation order to be specific, where it previously provided only for "reasonable visitation"
- make an order changing the custody of the child
- hold your former spouse in contempt of court
- reduce or withhold spousal or child support

Again, all these remedies depend on court orders. If you simply take unilateral action, such as not paying child support, you'll be hurting only yourself!

Taking a Child Out of State

Mrs. R. was awarded custody of the two children and $100 a month child support. Mr. R. received reasonable visitation on alternate weekends. Shortly thereafter, Mrs. R. moved to Nevada, concealed her address, and successfully prevented Mr. R.'s visitation rights. Mr. R. deposited the monthly child support in a bank trust account, then sought a change of custody order.

Mr. R. was awarded custody of the two children on the grounds that the mother had "sabotaged" his visitation rights, and he had not withheld child support payments.

In most instances, a final divorce decree specifies that the custodial parent is not to remove the children from the jurisdiction of the court (usually from the state) without permission of the court. This protects the visitation rights of the non-custodial parent.

On the other hand, a custodial parent may, for proper reasons, remove a child from the state where the divorce occurred, even though from a practical viewpoint that may frustrate the other parent's visitation rights.

Kelly was divorced in Philadelphia and was awarded custody of his child. His wife was ordered to pay child support for a limited time and was granted visitation rights. When Kelly finished grad school, he applied for and received permission from the court to move to Atlanta with his daughter to take a job there. His wife objected that she couldn't visit the child in Atlanta. The judge affirmed his ruling that Kelly could move — under the circumstances — even though it frustrated his wife's visitation rights.

The above example illustrates the wisdom of getting permission from the court before you make such a move. As part of the procedure, you must give the judge enough information to reassure him or her that your plan is not merely to frustrate your ex-wife's visitation rights. In short, go to the judge with places, dates, numbers, reasons, and so on.

What to Do If Your Child Is Abused or Neglected by the Mother

In January, when Dan took his son to the movies on a scheduled visitation, he noticed the boy was bruised and cut. The boy seemed unwilling to talk about it but said it didn't hurt. Later, Dan's former wife said the boy had fallen down.

In March, on a visit, Dan again noticed that his son limped. On examination of the boy, Dan discovered welts on the boy's thighs and backside. Again, the boy was unwilling to discuss how it happened.

Unless Dan has good reason to conclude that both incidents were truly accidental, he'd better have the boy examined by a physician, who may be able to give him a professional opinion (that will be admissible in court) as to whether the boy's condition was the result of abuse. If so, of course, Dan will immediately request a change of custody.

Dan should also notify his local child protective services if the doctor verifies the abuse. In short, Dan should start collecting *proof* of what apparently happened and let the mother worry about rebutting this proof.

When Ken takes his five-year-old daughter home after visitation, no one is home. It is dark and Ken takes his daughter back to his place after leaving a note. This is the third or fourth time this has happened. One time his former wife was pretty drunk when he returned his daughter.

Again, if these incidents appear to be accidental and unlikely to be repeated, Ken should give the mother hell and see what happens next time. But if you are convinced that it simply would not be right to leave your child with his or her mother, or if the mother is not home when you return and this is a pattern, take some action.

Call the police, if necessary, as well as the child protective services, and report the incident before taking the child home with you. Again, you'll collect some proof to offer the judge when you request a change of custody.

Similarly, if you are the custodial parent and your former wife returns from visitation with your kid and you suspect there has been mistreatment of some sort involved, call your attorney and have him or her request the court to deny further visitation. Do not attempt to terminate the visitation on your own unless the child appears to be in serious and immediate danger.

16
Changing Child Custody, Support, or Visitation Orders

Child custody, support, and visitation are determined when the divorce is final, either by court judgment or by an agreement of the husband and wife that then becomes part of the judgment.

However, the domestic relations court retains what is called "continuing jurisdiction" over the persons involved, which is a different procedure from that used in other civil actions. This means that the same court judge has the power to *change* its orders or judgments for custody, support, or visitation, provided a change is justified and necessary. Such a change is called "modification" of the order or judgment.

As far as orders regarding children are concerned, any proposed change is examined by the same standard used to make the original orders, namely, will the change be in the best interests of the child?

Ben's former wife was awarded custody of their son Michael even though Ben was a devoted and excellent father. Michael now is alone every afternoon after school and spends most nights with a babysitter. The boy is failing in his grades, is in poor health, and has recently been picked up by the juvenile authorities.

On the basis of these facts, it would clearly be in the boy's best interests to transfer his custody to Max.

But what about a situation where the best interests of the parent seem to be the chief concern?

John was ordered to pay $300 a month child support, based on his income from his business. When the credit crunch hit, John's business was hurt badly, and his income is now a fourth of what it was.

John may be granted a reduction in his child support obligation because of his changed circumstances. The best interests of his child are still the determining standard, but now those best interests are examined in the light of the father's new circumstances.

Sometimes the proposed change is justified because of the change in circumstances of the other party:

Dick was ordered to pay $200 a month child support, based on his earnings as a mailman. At the time of his divorce, his wife was unemployed. Dick still earns about the same, but his wife now makes more than he does.

Again a reduction in Dick's support payments may be justified — not because of his changed circumstances but because of his wife's.

Note: Where a change in custody is requested and granted, a change in child support and visitation rights is also required.

When Marty was divorced, his wife was awarded custody of their son. Marty was ordered to pay child support and given reasonable visitation. Marty's ex-wife now leaves the boy with Marty for long periods. This time he has been with Marty for two months, and Marty learns that she has quit her job and is spending the child support money on a lover.

Obviously, Marty should contact his lawyer immediately and seek a change in all three orders — custody, support, and visitation. When Marty makes his application for these changes, the judge will probably decide to grant his application because it is in the best interests of the boy to live with his father.

On the other hand:

At the time of divorce, Ed was an accountant making $4,000 a month. His wife had an income of $500 a month. Ed was ordered to pay $450 a month child support.
Ed lost his job and now teaches school, making $2,000 a month. His former wife's income has risen to $1,500 a month.

On the basis of these facts, only one order is in question — that of support. An adjustment in this order probably will not affect the custody or visitation orders.

By Agreement

You and your former wife can save a lot of time and money by *agreeing* to changes in custody, support, or visitation that are reasonable under the changed circumstances. Your agreement will usually be approved by the judge, provided it assures the welfare of the child. In effect, the private agreement of the parties involved is an informal modification of the court's orders. Neither parent need hire a lawyer, and a lot of ill will on everyone's part is avoided.

Carlos, an engineer, was awarded custody of his daughter at the divorce. He and his former wife are both fond of the girl, and although joint custody wouldn't work, they cooperate well in planning for her future.

Carlos left his daughter with his former wife when he left the country on an assignment in South America. His future work plans are uncertain. His former wife requests that custody of the daughter be given to her.

If there are no complications, such as support or visitation problems, Carlos and his former wife should try to make an agreement changing custody of their daughter to her mother. In the agreement, of course, both parents must provide for child support by Carlos as well as his specific visitation rights. Each parent should keep a copy of the agreement and file the original in the court that made the divorce decree or judgment.

It is very common for divorced parents to change the court order by mutual agreement and never bother to put the agreement in writing and file it in court. For example:

Judith was awarded custody of her and Pete's son. She then had an opportunity to go to Europe for several years to further her profession. She and Pete agreed that he will keep their boy indefinitely, and she will send money for support as needed. This arrangement has worked well for some time now.

Perhaps it is wise to leave a good thing alone, but we feel that both Judith and Pete (as well as their boy) will be better off writing out the agreement, filing it in court, and obtaining the judge's approval. The boy may become ill and need hospitalization, which will require the consent of his custodial parent. A school may need the authorization of a guardian. Pete may have an accident and be unable to care for the boy. Or Pete and Judith simply may change their minds later on. The moral? *If you agree, put it in writing.*

When to Call a Lawyer   In many instances, writing up your own agreement for a change in child custody, support, or visitation is pennywise and pound foolish. A change in custody and support, for example, may involve important tax considerations for one or both parents. There may be certain technical requirements in your state that apply to such agreements and how they must be filed in court. You may have a problem with ambiguous language that will produce uncertainties later on about what you both meant.

If you have any doubts, call your lawyer. Unless you and your former wife differ enormously on what you want, the lawyer should be able to write up the agreement for a couple of hundred dollars (or even less in many cases). He or she will also advise you as to where and when to file the agreement and how to obtain the judge's approval. It probably will be worth it, just for the peace of mind.

Remember that in any event the alternative to agreement is another court hearing, together with attorney's fees, costs, and the possibility of losing.

For those men who want to draw up their own agreement for a change in custody, support, or visitation, here is a checklist of matters that should be covered:

Change of Custody
  • the provisions of the original decree or order awarding custody
  • the change in circumstances that justify a change
  • the parent that will have custody under the agreement
  • new provisions for child support
  • new provisions for visitation
  • a statement that the new custodial parent may (or may not) move to another area with the child
  • a statement that the new custodial parent may (or may not) raise the child as he or she sees fit
  • a provision as to how long the agreement is to last (until the child is of age, for example)

- who is to decide future disputes under the agreement (judge, court conciliation, or whatever)
- who is to pay any costs involved
- the date the agreement is to be filed in court
- a provision for rewriting the agreement in the event that it is not approved by the judge

Change of Child Support

- the provisions of the original decree concerning support
- who pays and who receives the support (for the child)
- the present amount and method of payment
- the new amount and method of payment
- a statement generally giving the reasons for the change (loss of employment, change in income, and the like)
- new tax provisions (for example, who has the deduction)
- the duration of the agreement
- a statement that the agreement will be filed in court by a given date

Change in Visitation Rights

- the provisions of the original decree as to visitation
- the circumstances giving rise to the change (for example, if the father cannot visit on weekdays)
- the new visitation arrangements (time, place, conditions)
- who is to pay any costs involved (for travel, child transportation, and the like)
- the duration of the agreement
- a statement that the agreement is to be filed in court by a given date

Note: Your state may have additional requirements for changing original decrees by agreement. Be sure to check with the clerk of the domestic relations department in your court before you try to file an agreement of *any* kind.

By Court Hearing

A change in an original court order for custody, child support, or visitation rights is usually obtained in open court by what lawyers call a "motion." A motion in this context means a request made to the judge, supported by evidence (including argument). A lawyer is not required but is recommended, since the proceeding is fairly technical. However, if you have very clear grounds for the change, such as abandonment by the mother, you may represent yourself adequately with a little help. We suggest you contact an organization such as Equal Rights for Fathers, Men's Rights, or even NOW (National Organization for Women). The latter has been helpful to men's causes on various occasions.

The other parent — the one against whom the change is being sought — has a right to be heard in court in his or her defense. Otherwise, a parent could be deprived of his or her legal rights without "due process." However, due process does *not* mean that in every case a parent's right to custody, for example, must be determined before the child's custody can be changed. For example, a child may be taken from his or her custodial parent in a quick legal proceeding (called a "summary proceeding"), provided the parent may later have his or her rights determined.

Bob finds his daughter ill and malnourished when he arrives for his visitation. The mother has left without explanation, and Bob finds out that she has left the state. Bob has a good chance of obtaining custody of his daughter in a summary proceeding, provided the custodial mother's rights are determined later.

The courts in some states refuse to accept and enforce child custody decrees entered by courts in other states. This leads to what lawyers call "forum shopping" by non-custodial parents who seek to change the decree. This practice has led to the enactment of a law called the Uniform Child Custody Jurisdiction Act.

The states that have adopted this act are:

Alaska	Indiana	North Dakota
California	Iowa	Ohio
Colorado	Maryland	Oregon
Delaware	Michigan	Pennsylvania
Florida	Minnesota	Wisconsin
Hawaii	Montana	Wyoming
Idaho	New York	

The act prevents forum shopping and provides that a court in one state cannot change a custody decree that has been made by another state, subject to certain technical exceptions.

248

Strategy

The most important thing to remember when you appear in court to change an order or decree is that *the judge has heard the case once*. And judges hate to decide the same question twice — in fact, they won't. If you're planning to rehash old issues and arguments, forget it.

For example, when a judge is asked for a second time to determine who should have custody of the children, he or she will only listen to evidence showing that circumstances have changed since the original order.

At the original custody hearing, both you and your wife presented the judge with facts regarding the suitability of each of you to be the custodial parent. And the relevant witnesses have already testified — child custody investigators, psychologists, and so on. You will *not* be permitted to give the same evidence again, even if it has a slightly different slant.

Changed Circumstances: What Are They?

The law in virtually every state provides that custody, child support, or visitation orders or judgments may be modified only when a change of circumstances justifies such a change, and the change will be in the best interests of the child.

One judge, commenting on changes of custody, remarked:

[Some] authority can be found on both sides of nearly every contention that can be made for changing or not changing the custody of a child.

[Stack vs. Stack, 1961, 189 CA2d 357]

The judge was right. Fathers and mothers seeking changes of court orders regarding children and their welfare have come up with just about every reason imaginable. Some are frivolous and asserted only to harass the other parent. Others, however, are serious and require a judge to listen carefully and weigh the respective merits of the positions.

Some generalizations:
 • The change in circumstances must be substantial, not trivial.

- The change in circumstances must have been unforeseen at the time the judge made the original order or decree (an increase in the cost of living, for example, would be foreseen).
- The change must be in the best interests of the child.

Changes in Custody

There is simply no fixed standard by which you can decide what constitutes the kind of change in circumstances that will justify a change in a custody order.

Obviously, the death of the custodial parent is a critical change in circumstances. In fact, in many states a change in the custody decree is not even required; the surviving parent's right to custody of the children is automatic. The insanity of the custodial parent is a similarly substantial change in circumstances.

Other than the above, what kinds of acts by your former wife might justify a change in custody to you? Or, what kinds of acts by you may justify a change of custody to your former wife?

Personal Behavior   A change in custody is frequently sought by the non-custodial parent on the ground that the custodial parent's personal behavior or habits are harmful to the child's welfare. As would be expected, this covers a variety of evils and is very difficult to prove or disprove. Often, such grounds are alleged because of religious or moral differences between the parents that have little to do with the child's actual welfare. However, sometimes a very real danger is involved.

Roger, in an Ohio case, proved that the custodial mother of his eight-year-old son had been arrested twice for drunkenness and once for possession of drugs. On this evidence alone, the court modified the prior order and awarded Roger custody of the boy.

In a Pennsylvania case, evidence showed that the custodial mother of a thirteen-year-old daughter had become physically disabled, was living with a homosexual companion, and that the daughter was becoming addicted to alcohol. A change in custody to the father was granted.

However:

A non-custodial father alleged and proved, in a Missouri court, that the custodial mother of his eight-year-old son used marijuana and alcohol to excess. The court held that in the absence of evidence that the mother's conduct was practiced in the home and was harmful to the child's welfare, the father's request for a change of custody would be denied.

In California, Ken requested a change of custody for his twelve-year-old son, alleging and proving that the custodial mother had various men in her home on an overnight basis. His request was denied. There was no evidence that the mother's conduct in the son's presence was other than proper, or that her private conduct harmed her son's welfare.

The reasons given for a change in court order are limited only by people's ingenuity, but the following reasons have been accepted in actual court cases. Remember when reading this list, though, that each case is judged *on its own facts.* Few workable generalizations can do more than guide you as to what judges have accepted in other cases.

- the inability of the child to get along where he or she is
- to provide a more stable home relationship and a better sense of moral values (such as religious affiliations where the child's background was religious)
- changes in the health or emotional well being of the custodial parent
- misrepresentation of facts at the original hearing by the custodial parent
- estranging the child from the visiting parent by poisoning his or her mind
- unauthorized removal of the child from the state by the custodial parent
- lack of care for the child resulting in his or her illness or neglect
- denial of or interference with the visitation rights of the non-custodial parent
- abusiveness to the child by the custodial parent
- excessive drinking, use of drugs, or promiscuous sexual behavior by the custodial parent
- the infliction of unreasonable punishment on the child by the custodial parent

- the failure of the custodial parent to provide necessaries for the child
- abandonment of the child
- the ability of the non-custodial parent to provide a good home, if his or her former inability was due to facts that have changed
- the poor health or physical condition of the custodial parent

Custody of children is *not* changed because of:
- immorality
- occasional excessive drinking
- the bad character or disposition of the custodial parent
- failure to pay debts or financial failure
- past indiscretions

What If You Re-Marry Your "Ex"?   Suppose that custody of the children of your marriage is awarded to one of you upon divorce and you later marry your former partner again. In this case, the custody order is inoperative. However, if the custody of the children has been awarded to a third party, your remarriage does not affect the order.

Child Support

If you are a father seeking to reduce child support previously ordered by the court, you must be able to prove that circumstances have changed — either with you or your former wife — and justify such a reduction.

As stated before, a predictable cost of living increase in your own expenses or maintenance is *not* an unforeseen event that will justify a reduction. Nor is the fact that you have voluntarily quit your job and are presently unemployed, unless you quit because you lost your ability to perform.

In order to be successful in your request that your present obligation be reduced (or even terminated), you must be prepared to prove one or more of the following:
- You are unemployed or have reduced income due to no fault of your own.

- You have suffered unanticipated financial reverses because of illness, injury, or loss of property.
- Where appropriate, you have remarried and have incurred additional obligations.
- Where appropriate, your former wife has remarried.
- Your child has increased income or has an increased ability to earn income.
- Your former wife's income has increased substantially.
- The needs of your child have been reduced.

Generally, the following circumstances will *not* justify a reduction in your child support payments:

- You are unemployed or have reduced income because of your own acts.
- You are living with another woman and have incurred additional expenses.
- The cost of living has increased.
- Your own needs have increased.
- The custodial mother's income has increased a modest amount.

When requesting that child support be reduced, remember that in many courts the judge will use a support chart or table as a handy reference for making the order. This table is a good guide as to how the judge will handle your request for a change. Ask the clerk of your family law court for a copy and study it.

Visitation

In a great number of cases, changing the frequency or place of visitation is worked out informally by the parents where circumstances have changed.

Under the divorce decree, Keith is entitled to visit his son Don every other weekend and for one month in the summer. Keith now works weekends, and his former wife is a nurse and works the weekday shift. They agree that Keith will pick up the boy on Wednesdays and return him on Friday mornings.

Keith and his former wife probably shouldn't bother with a formal change in the original visitation order. The circumstances might change again soon, or they might decide that other weekdays are better for his visitation.

In many cases, though, the parents cannot agree and modification of the visitation agreement order must be sought in court.

By agreement, Janet was entitled to visitation rights with her son for a week at Christmas and a month in the summer. The boy has now been sent to a private school and is no longer free during those periods. If Janet and her former husband can't agree on a new visitation plan, she should request a modification of the original agreement.

Remember that if your visitation rights are frustrated by the custodial mother or if she has estranged the child from you to such a degree that normal visitation is impossible, a change in visitation is not what you need. You should request a change in custody on the ground that your former spouse has violated the visitation order.

Note also that your visitation rights may be suspended or even terminated if you are substantially in arrears in your child support payments. If you are requesting a change in visitation rights, be sure you are current in any child support obligation. Otherwise the judge probably won't even hear your case.

Attorney's Fees

There is considerable work for an attorney representing anyone seeking changes in a court order. In addition to the technical requirements of notice, motions, and so on, a substantial amount of time must be spent in most cases digging up legal proof to support the client's position. Our guess is that in a contested case of average difficulty, a lawyer will charge you from $500–$2,000.

The court costs should run about $50–$100, depending on where you live. Don't be too dismayed by all of this. If you have a good case for a change of order and are successful, the courts in most states have the power to award you attorney's fees and costs (the same is true, of course, of your wife).

Appendix:
Men's Rights Organizations

Groups organized to promote men's legal interests are beginning to come into existence. These groups are not comparable in power to most of the well-established women's rights organizations; nevertheless they might be able to provide you with advice and help with your specific problems.

Organizations Promoting Men's Interests Generally

Men International
P.O. Box 189
Forest Lake, Minnesota 55025
(612) 464-7663
R. F. Doyle, Chairman

The 3,000-member Men's Rights Association is part of Men International.

Men's Liberation
c/o Mr. Frank Karian
New York Life Insurance Co.
350 Fifth Avenue
New York, New York 10001
(212) 563-5900
Frank Karian, Executive Director

This organization is "militantly" committed to men getting a better deal in alimony, and advocates equalized child support obligations.

Society of Dirty Old Men
Box 88385
Indianapolis, Indiana 46208
David L. Palmer, Executive Officer

This 18,000-strong organization is dedicated to humor and male supremacy. It publishes a newsletter and *Every Male's Guide to Chauvinism.*

Organizations Concerned with Divorce and Child Custody

Adam and Eve
1008 White Oak
Arlington Heights, Illinois 60005
(312) 394-1040
Donna Brockman, Secretary

This organization advocates divorce reform and has 7,000 members. Counseling and legal referrals provided. Newsletter.

America's Society of Divorced Men (ASDM)
575 Keep Street
Elgin, Illinois 60120
(312) 695-2200

An organization for divorced and separated men. The objective is to assist men in fighting the "divorce racket." It advocates establishing respect for marriage in the courts and strengthening the rights of fathers.

Committee for Fair Divorce and Alimony Laws
Box 641
Lenox Hill Station
New York, New York 10021
George Dunbar, President

This 2,000-strong organization is composed of individuals who want change in the "antiquated" divorce and alimony laws of New York and elsewhere. It advocates both parents having equal custody, support, and visitation rights. Publishes monthly newsletter. Formed the Institute for the Study of Matrimonial Law (see below).

Institute for the Study of Matrimonial Law
c/o Sidney Siller
370 Lexington Avenue
New York, New York 10017
(212) 682-1043
Sidney Siller, President

Studies the legal and emotional aspects of divorce. Publishes monthly bulletins.

Divorce Aid, Inc.
9101 Pelican Avenue
Fountain Valley, California 92708
(714) 968-2973
Clint Jones, Director

This is a self-help organization providing emotional "first aid" following divorce or separation. Referral service. Affiliated with MEN (Male Equity Now, Inc.).

Equal Rights for Fathers
P.O. Box 6327
Albany, California 94706
(415) 848-2323

This is a non-profit organization dedicated to equal justice for all in family law cases; it is especially concerned with fair child custody and visitation, free of sex bias and other abuses. Provides referral service and "aid and assistance sessions."

United States Divorce Reform (USDR)
P.O. Box 243
Kenwood, California 95452
(707) 833-2550
George Partes, Director

This organization advocates removing divorce proceedings from the court and non-adversary methods of ending marriages, for example, arbitration.

Bibliography

Books

Atkin, Edith, and Rubin, Estelle. *Part-Time Father*. Vanguard Press, 1976.

Biller, Henry. *Paternal Deprivation*. Lexington Books, 1975.

Cassidy, Robert. *What Every Man Should Know About Divorce*. New Republic, 1977.

Corman, Avery. *Kramer vs. Kramer*. Signet, 1976.

Gatley, Richard H. *Single Father's Handbook*. Anchor Press/Doubleday, 1979.

Glieberman, Herbert A. *Confessions of a Divorce Lawyer*. Ballantine, 1975.

Goldberg, Herb. *The Hazards of Being Male: Surviving the Myth of Masculine Privilege*. Signet, 1976.

Goldstein, Joseph. *Beyond the Best Interests of the Child*. The New York Free Press, 1973.

Green, Maureen. *Fathering*. McGraw-Hill Paperbacks, 1978.

Hunt, Morton and Bernice. *The Divorce Experience*. McGraw-Hill, 1977.

Ihara, Toni, and Warner, Ralph. *The Living Together Kit*. Nolo Press, 1979.

Levine, James. *Who Will Raise the Children? New Options for Fathers (and Mothers)*. Bantam, 1976.

Nichols, Jack. *Men's Liberation*. Penguin, 1976.

Marvin, Albert. *One Man, Hurt*. Random House, 1978.

Rheinstein, Max. *Marriage, Stability, Divorce and the Law*. University of Chicago Press, 1972.

Roman, Mel, and Haddad, William. *The Disposable Parent: The Case for Joint Custody.* Penguin Books, 1978.

Sheresky, Norman, and Mannes, Marian. *Uncoupling: The Art of Coming Apart.* The Viking Press, 1972.

Stafford, Linley M. *One Man's Family.* Random House, 1978.

Weiss, Robert S. *Marital Separation.* Basic Books, 1975.

Victor, Ira, and Winkler, Ann. *Fathers and Custody.* Hawthorn Books, 1977.

Newsletters

Hirschfeld, Bob, editor. *Single Dad's Lifestyle.* Phoenix Rising Publications, P.O. Box 4842, Scottsdale, AZ 85258.

Pasco, Richard, editor. *Equal Rights for Fathers Newsletter.* Equal Rights for Fathers, P.O. Box 6327, Albany, CA 94706.

Index